MW01274999

MEET THE PASTOR'S WIFE

By

Nichelle Williams Isiah

COPYRIGHT

Copyright © 2021 by Nichelle Isiah

All rights reserved. No part of this publication may be reproduced, distributed, or transmitted in any form or by any means, including photocopying, recording, or other electronic, mechanical methods, without the prior written permission of the author, except in the case of brief quotations embodied in critical reviews and certain other noncommercial uses permitted by copyright law. For permission requests, write to the author at the address below.

Nichelle Isiah

nichelleisiah8@gmail.com

Printed in the United States

DEDICATIONS

CHURCH MOTHER'S BOOK DEDICATION

Honoring and Introducing

My Own Church Mother, a "Lady" Indeed!

Mother Mary Joyce Manning/Texas

*M*other Mary Manning is Church Mother of the Salvation Lighthouse Church, located in Mexia, Texas. Lovely in her presentation and in the way she treats the people she meets, she is one who is in love with Jesus and reflects the image of Christ! As we feel a Church Mother should, Mother Manning shows us love and how to love. "She is wise, compassionate, and possesses a Godly reverence. She both models and teaches acceptable behavior." We at Salvation Lighthouse recognize that we have a 'Precious Jewel' and so many others who know her realize and love her too!

I have often watched her; she has a Holy Spirit calming effect about herself. She speaks peace to situations around her; there is a way she addresses circumstances, and that is by way of the Anointing!

Mother Mary Joyce Gatson Manning is a "Lady."

She was born in Fairfield, Texas, and her late husband was a Pastor and Superintendent (Pastor of Pastors). Together they ministered in and to various Church congregations and were married 58 years.

Mother Manning seems to beam and glow with admiration as she speaks of Superintendent Lenard James Manning. She says of him, "He was tall and very handsome; and used to be the lead singer of a gospel quartet group out of Fort Hood, TX."

Mother Manning spoke to me with transparency as she said that over time, she learned to pray about the overzealous women who at times seemed to overstep their bounds and were vying for the attention of her husband. Mother Manning says God helped her with anger because she didn't like it one bit, and she learned to discuss certain things that bothered her with her husband.

She says, when her husband became sickly, she cared for him herself. She loved him, and this was her "Labor of Love." Mother Manning remembers with joy how he would take her on road trips. There were places he wanted her to see, and he would keep her dressed pretty.

Mother Manning is the mother of five adult children, four of which serve at Salvation Lighthouse Church. Their sons are in place, carrying on the ministry there. In Spiritual leadership, her sons, Pastor Don, Sr., and Minister Richard, Assistant Pastor, are their anointed wives beside them. (They are "Ladies," and you can read about them in their respective chapters – Lady Tina Manning and Lady Dianne Manning). This is a family unit that works together for the cause of Christ. Her two beautiful daughters and their supportive husbands are right there serving the Lord, in the beauty of Holiness, as well. You can tell that Lady Manning and her Late husband, the Pastor raised their children well (to God be the glory).

Mother Manning would leave words of encouragement for the Pastor's wives:
She shared,

> *It's a journey. Being a Minister's Wife is a journey, and you have*
> *to be patient; you can't quit! It makes the Wife look bad when she*
> *quits. You've got a job to do, and the #1 job is praying for your*
> *husband. Every Pastor doesn't know how to talk to people.*

It's her place to help him with that. You get home and mention, for example: "Honey, what you said was right, but it was the way you said it," and such.

LEADING LADY'S BOOK DEDICATION
Recognizing and Presenting

My Former First Lady

Lady Mary Davis/Washington State

$\mathcal{T}$he Leading Lady of the Eastside Assembly of Believers Church of God in Christ, **Missionary Mary L. Davis,** has accomplished many things in her life. She has supported Superintendent Emeritus Alfred C. Davis, Sr. as a Wife, business, and ministerial partner for over 43 years. She continues to be an influential leader in the Church and the local community.

She has led and operated extensions of the Church, such as the Alpha House (a drug and alcohol facility) and a thrift store. She also had a career in the federal government in its finance and accounting department.

She was the owner/director of the Koinonia Child Care Center for over ten years. This center was not just a place for business but also a place of ministry. Her business took a holistic approach in caring for children and their families. She realized that she couldn't be an effective witness for Christ unless she met the needs of the families who used her childcare center. Often, Missionary Davis gave food and clothing, provided advice and words of encouragement to parents.

She was also the president of the Tacoma Ministerial Alliance Wives. In June 2002, she received her missionary license from the Washington State Jurisdiction Churches of God in Christ.

In June 2003, she graduated from Pierce College with her associate degree in Early Childhood Development Center.

Missionary Davis has exemplified the definition of a "helpmeet" while creating her own identified legacy. She respects Pastor Davis as her husband and Spiritual leader and recognizes that God had a special purpose for her life. She has been victorious over the attacks of the enemy and refuses to give up as she knows that God is doing a mighty work in her. Through her praying, she has survived and overcome many obstacles, from poverty to beating cancer. She is a woman of great strength and courage.

IN LOVING MEMORY OF

My Late Grandmother (Big Momma)

First Lady, Lucille Williams Dawson/California

ut we do not want you to be uninformed, brothers and sisters, about those who are asleep, so that you will not grieve as indeed the rest of mankind do, who have no hope" 1 Thessalonians 4:13 (NASB).

My paternal grandmother, Lucille Williams Dawson, has been gone over 'yonder' for many years now, yet I had enough time around her as a little girl to remember her.

I remember this specific picture of her hanging in her living room on the wall. I often stared at this classic black 'n white photo as a child.

I remember she had the largest collection of Christmas greeting cards, literally strung across the wall. Even until now, I have not seen anyone receive so many greeting cards on any one holiday. Grandma, in my opinion, was very well known.

I remember the beautiful blossoming pink roses that covered a portion of the white picket fence in front of Grandma's house, which is probably the reason I love flowers today.

I remember, at Church and the state jurisdictional meetings (California NW region of Churches), that Grandma had her tambourine and wore stiletto heels. A child notices things about people, and these things and more, I noticed of her. *(I today love my tambourine, but not so much into stilettos).*

I remember the black, upright piano (yes, very much an antique). It had once been a player piano. Years after *Big Momma* passed, I was blessed to have had it in my home for years. After seeing it for so many years as a child in her home, it was a pleasure to have it in mine. I had full intention of having this piano fully restored one day. *What happened? Well, it's a long story to be told another time.*

My grandmother was also a "Lady." My paternal Grandfather was a Pastor and Superintendent (Pastor of Pastors). She was his bride, a Pastor's Wife. I was too young to even think of asking her about that journey as we have asked First Ladies in this book endeavor, but I know she was with him until his passing.

I actually remember my parents taking me into her hospital room the day before she passed away. I knew she'd been sick and in my little girl's heart wanted to sing a song and encourage her.

I look forward to the great family reunion over there in glory with the Lord, one glad morning. For today, I am thankful for the opportunity to take space on paper to *'INTRODUCE TO MOST AND PRESENT TO MANY OTHERS,* my grandmother, aka 'Big Momma.' She was a **"LADY,"** or Mother Lucille Williams Dawson. What a blessing to remember and honor her memory in this way, as well.

(Pictured above, Big Momma and my cousins from the Bay Area)

ACKNOWLEDGMENTS

Special thanks and big hugs to my first cousin and editor.

Mrs. Marlene C Bertrand

For your editing needs contact her at:

Marlene@MarleneCBertrand.com

www.MarleneCBertrand.com (web)

Mrs. Jamie Mclean

Watercolor Painting

Groesbeck, TX Library Director

Thank you for the beautiful watercolor artwork.

It has been such a pleasure working with you.

jamiemcleanart@gmail.com

Salvation Lighthouse Church of God in Christ

Mexia, TX

Thank you for your loving support.

TABLE OF CONTENTS

NICHELLE'S NOTE - 1
The Bride's Bouquet

*W*hen was the last time you took the time to look at a bouquet of flowers? Maybe it was flowers you received from your loving significant other; maybe it was a Mother's Day floral gift. Even while shopping in my local Walmart store, I myself sometimes take the time to look at the bundles of flowers they have available. The colors are ever so vibrant: yellows, greens, purples, pinks, and more.

The beauty of one individual flower is majestic all by itself. The *awesome* creativity of our Lord is on display in the details of the colorful petals, the distinctively shaped leaves, and stems, whether they are in clusters or single, tall or short, so beautiful!!

I have read that there are over 400,000 types of flowering plants. Father God is such a brilliant creator, indeed! Lord, I give you praise!

Now you take these varying types of flowers with all their unique differences and put them together. You take a red rose, a yellow daffodil, white 'baby's breath,' and other of God's fragrant creation, and you have a bouquet! A handful of scented beauty!

Carried by a groom's bride, it is 'icing on the cake' let's face it, a woman and flowers is a classic and romantic concept that has been consistent through time.

We bring this concept to the Pastor's Wife, the overall celebrant of this specific writing. The Pastor's Wife is and was the radiant bride of the Pastor. 'Marriage is honorable before God,'

Refer to Hebrews 13:4-6 (KJV). It does not matter when they married, where they married, whether it was a big luxurious wedding event, a stand before the justice of the peace, or a highly anticipated destination wedding. If they legally married, he was the groom and she, the bride.

In "Meet the Pastor's Wife," we use this concept of the Bridal Bouquet to parallel the ornate beauty of each of the Pastor's Wives. Created in God's image, these are the 'Fearfully and wonderfully made' up of God. Like a flower, not one of these "Leading Ladies" is the same, and they aren't supposed to be. Each is unique! Her voice, her God-given giftings, and the way she ministers are different from another and differ even in how she dresses and styles her hair.

In this book, it is this that we strive to point out. As a part of the 'Body of Christ, ' these First Ladies, these Pastor's wives, make up a big, beautiful bouquet. They are scented with the glory of God, working together, binding together in God's love to **work the works of Him** who has sent the Body of Christ, as it says in John 9:4.

As brothers and sisters in Christ, let's recognize and celebrate God's floral shop and the "Feminine Graced" "Women of God" all around us. We are thankful for the beauty of God in all of God's servants. See the beauty, pray for, and celebrate the Pastor's Bride, aka the Pastor's Wife. She is the "Leading Lady" standing beside your Pastor, the "First Lady" working with him in the Gospel within our congregation. Do not compare her to another. She is who God says she is and, certainly, like those individual flowers together in a vase and carefully arranged, making a bouquet. God made these individuals just as BEAUTIFUL!

NICHELLE'S NOTE - 2
Many Hats, Many Titles <u>All</u> "LADIES"

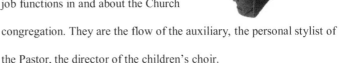

ow many of you Church folk know that 'Women of God, in general, wear many hats? Oh yes, they do, and if you didn't know, now you know! When I say "Hats," I mean that they work in

varying capacities and perform many job functions in and about the Church congregation. They are the flow of the auxiliary, the personal stylist of the Pastor, the director of the children's choir.

Sometimes they are the soloist before the Man of God preaches, or they may have to teach Bible study in the case of the Pastor's absence. They may do an impromptu "Welcome," or referee and help to calm confusion.

The prayer warrior in the background, the Pastor's right hand "Lady" on the "Preacha's" arm; these are the Pastor's wives, also known as "First Ladies" and more!

So many "Hats" and so many titles. Follow me, let's go over just a few of them:
First Lady, Elect Lady, Leading Lady, Pastor So 'n So, Co-Pastor So 'n So, Mother Founder, and more.

Mrs. (First name), Mrs. (Last name), Sister (First name), and Sister (Last name), and some are simply called by their first name: "Sally Sue, may I speak to you about getting some counseling?"

Oh, and the plot thickens (giggling out loud). I know of two Churches where either the Pastor or First Lady is referred to as "Honey." God bless them. They know who they are. I love y'all.

So, why did I bring all of this up? Because, after praying and getting the input of many of you "Ladies" out there, I decided on the overall title: **MEET THE PASTOR'S WIFE.** As an author, I made the decision to call everyone **A "LADY."**

In every aspect of the word, and I do say so with the highest regard, you all are "Ladies." Yes, I do realize that you all wear many hats - proverbially and have even bigger titles, and I want to respect and honor every single one of you and the title you serve with, but

FOR THE PURPOSE OF THIS BOOK, I went with the simplest way of handling all these proverbial "Hats." I decided to refer to all as "Lady."

 Occasionally, one or more of your other titles may be mentioned in writing. I aim to show no favoritism, and my goal is to refer to you all as the beautiful, Anointed "Lady" that you are. For those of you, my senior, and you're a seasoned "Mother in Zion," I have meant no harm to call you a Lady. If your testimony is being told here, the bottom line is that you are the Wife of a Pastor, or you once were. I just wanted to kindly give this DISCLAIMER so that all was understood, and the Blessed Overcoming Testimonials written in between the book cover would be received with love.

Love you,

Nichelle

THANK YOU FOR STANDING BESIDE MY PASTOR

*O*nce upon a time, I was in a military family. My then spouse was enlisted in the Army, and for several years we lived here and there! When 'Uncle Sam' said OK, it's time to change duty stations (called the PCS – permanent change of station), we were packed up and would move on. This PCS also meant that upon moving, we would have to find a new Church home, a new Pastor, which in most cases included meeting a "new" Pastor's Wife.

So, needless to say, I have had a few Pastors' wives to be involved in my life. Like a bouquet of flowers, each one has been different than the other. A better word to describe it is 'unique,' and so I take the time and space on this paper to **'INTRODUCE TO SOME AND PRESENT TO OTHERS'** the following First Ladies from past and present. Two of them have passed over to her reward, and the rest continue to be in Christ's service in their respective places.

- *Thank you, first ladies, for the love and attention you showed my family and me.*
- *Thank you for sharing your husband with us as our Pastor.*
- *Thank you for your smile, your hug, your teaching, and your example in "feminine grace." I recognize God's grace on your life, and I have seen the anointing of God operating in you.*
- *Thank you for every sacrifice you have ever made to enrich the Church congregation. Thank you, thank you, thank you!*

11

I RECOGNIZE AND HONOR

- *My own Grandmother*: *The Late Lady Lucille Williams Dawson from California (see in memory of page)*

- *My own Mother*: *Lady Lois Marie Williams from California (see CHAPTER 22)*

- *Lady Patricia Matthews* / *Times of Refreshing Church from California (see CHAPTER TWO)*

- *Lady Diana Sapp* / *Antioch Church from Germany*

- *The Late Lady Anna M. Cook* / *New Birth Church from Tennessee*

- *Lady Barbara Washington* / *Holy Ghost Corner Church from Hawaii*

- *Lady Vivian Brooks* / *Holy Ghost Corner Church from Hawaii*

- *Lady Mary Davis* / *Eastside Church from Washington State*

- *Lady Linda Wright* / *Evangelic Temple Church from Tennessee*

- *Lady Wanda Gaines* / *Greater New Birth Church from Tennessee*

- *Lady Barbara Butler* / *Sweet Haven Church from New York*

- *Lady (Dr.) Jennifer Adebanjo* / *The Living Word Int'l Church from Tennessee*

- *Lady Denise Rease* / *Bible Way Church from New York*

- *Lady Gwendolyn Washington* / *Haynes Memorial Church from Texas*

- *Lady Tina Manning* / *Salvation Lighthouse Church from Texas*

OTHER BOOKS BY AUTHOR
NICHELLE WILLIAMS ISIAH
(All Available On Amazon)

- ARROW IN MY HEART…A WOMAN'S JOURNEY THROUGH MOTHERHOOD

- "ROUTE EIGHT – RADIO CHECK" … Sweet School Bus Stories and a Bumpy Ride

- THE MOM 'N POPS SURVIVAL GUIDE SERIES, (BOOK #1), STORMS ARE COMING,

  PREPARE!

CHAPTER ONE

Lady Patricia Matthews/California

*C*rust in the Lord with all your heart and lean not on your own understanding; 6 In all your ways acknowledge Him, And He shall [a]direct your paths" Proverbs 3:5-6 NKJV.

In this chapter of "Meet the Pastor's Wife," I may introduce to some and present to others: **Mother Patricia Matthews**, a native of Oakland and Merced, California, and presently living in the Fresno, CA area.

Proverbs 3:5-6 is her favorite scripture, and she says in her own words the reason is: "This scripture talks about putting your trust in the Lord and leaning not to your own understanding. This scripture has sustained me through the good and the bad." Lady Matthews explains.

I have known Mother Patricia Matthews for years now; during my college years, I was honored she was my Pastor's Wife; and my first real experience with a Pastor's Wife other than my own mother. Knowing her has been a pleasurable experience, and over the years, I can certainly say I have seen God's radiant glory through her.

The Times of Refreshing Church in Merced, CA, where both she and her husband and Pastor served, was a place for me of Spiritual growth, grace, and laughter. In my estimation, the median age of our congregation was about 30 at that time (I was straight from high school and happy to think I was now grown). Honestly, I was far from being fully mature, and in hindsight, God would use this congregation and Pastoring couple to impart many life lessons to me.

If I were to choose three words that would describe what I learned in this congregation, it would be "Word," "Worship," and "Laughter." Respectfully, this congregation had a Spirit of laughter. The Pastor, the First Lady, and the congregation, so many of us 30 years and younger, seemed to find

16

everything so funny. In my college years in Merced, I can honestly say that I learned how to see the lighthearted part of things. After all, Proverbs 17:22 says, "Laughter is medicine." It is there, at the Times of Refreshing Church, where I learned "Word" more of the Word of God! Lady Patricia Matthews was, and is, an integral part of this Church congregation, though they are now located in Fresno, CA.

Lady Matthews sings with a strong contralto voice, and even before I moved out of my parent's home to the small city of Merced, I'd seen her take command of their choir and, in my own words, bring out the best in their united voices. I'd be sitting at a revival, the 'Times of Refreshing' choir would be called up, and yes, the anointing would come in, those of us in the pews were now on our feet; sure, enough that choir had been used of God to lead us into praise 'n worship! There was her son on the drums, her husband (our Pastor) either on the keyboard or guitar, and Minister Larry (their brother) on the keyboard, as well. A musical family indeed, they are anointed to minister in music and God's Word. I was blessed to one day be a part of this choir and congregation, as well. This was the Church I attended while in college, and I have very fond memories of it all.

Pastor Johnny Matthews, Lady Matthews' husband, and Pastor were also the State Evangelists, so our Church congregation was mobile a lot. We had cars and vans full of excited people following our Pastor as he spoke God's Word at various Churches up and down the San Joaquin Valley of CA. I didn't realize it at the time, but I was learning how to support my Pastoral leadership with my presence as a part of the choir in song. Though I was a young college student with little money, my mama had already taught me to separate my tithing and offering to support a place that definitely supported me in so many different ways. These people will always be family to me, and my memories are packed full of laughter and love from my days with the *Times of Refreshing Church* family there (in Merced, CA.) at the time.

17

[NICHELLE'S NOTE – 3] *This Church is now located in Fresno, CA, in case you want to visit them.*

Speaking of music, song, and worship, Mother Matthews's two favorite songs are *Changed* by Chrystal Rucker and *Find A Way* By Brian Courtney Heal.

In knowing Lady Matthews, you'll hear her jovial laugh even to this day, every so often. It is a part of her personality, and I love it. She is down-to-earth, easy to converse with, and kind-hearted to boot!

Let's come in closer and hear more of her story from her own mouth.

"I came to know Christ at an early age through a friend of my mother, but I didn't accept Him until I was in the 9th grade under the leadership of Pastor Charles H. Webb." Lady Matthews says when asked about how she came to know Jesus.

"I met my husband when I was in high school. I had previously walked away from God during my last two years of high school. In my own mindset then, I wanted to do my own thing. In making this decision, I didn't want anyone to approach me about Church." Mother Matthews goes on and tells her story.

"This young man had moved in from Mississippi and eventually to Oakland, CA. As much as I tried to avoid Church people, I kept running into them, especially him. We went to the same high school. Our families lived down the street from each other, and the Church building was right on the corner near my parent's house. I would try to avoid him following me to school because he would talk about the things I was doing and would always mention JESUS!

18

"My now husband and Pastor had become the youth Pastor of the Church my cousins attended. There was a revival to begin, and I wanted to get them to leave me alone, so I went. It was on this particular night that he (my future husband) preached out of the book of Judges from the passage of scripture that says: 'The fool has said in his heart that there is no God' Psalm 14:1 (KJV). The title of his message was: 'He Died Like a Fool.' On this particular night of the revival service, many came to the Lord, and I was one of them. I just didn't want Jesus to come and catch me in my sins."

Did you ever envision that one day you would be a Pastor's Wife? And was it what you would have thought the role would be?

"No, I never envisioned myself being married to a preacher, but I was blessed to have a woman in my life who was my Pastor's Wife. I watched her closely, she had a Spirit about her that drew people, and she knew how to encourage you. There was an anointing about her. Many of the sisters modeled after her."

> *No, I never envisioned myself being married to a preacher; but I was blessed to have a woman in my life who was my Pastor's Wife. I watched her closely, she had a Spirit about her that drew people, and she knew how to encourage you. There was an anointing about her. Many of the sisters modeled after her.*

How long have you served in the role of the Pastor's Wife?

"I now have served in this role for 38 years and counting." Lady Matthews, at this point, has been married to her husband, the Pastor and Superintendent (Pastor overseeing other Pastors), for 50 years. Over time, First Lady Matthews has also been known as Mother Matthews (which honors her Spiritual maturity and service over several years). She also wears the hat of and serves as the Northern Regional Chairperson, a place of supervising among a grouping of Churches."

If your Church congregation were to send you and your husband on an all-expense-paid vacation to anywhere, where would you want to go?

"Italy or Hawaii."

What are some of the challenges you have encountered during this time as a Pastor's Wife?

"Being able to communicate with my husband about the vision God has given. What is my role? Finding my place, how to deal with people He has placed in the ministry," Lady Matthews answers."

Would you mind giving us some of the joys you have experienced in the role of being married to a Pastor?

"Traveling, ministering, preaching the Word of God, watching God perform healings and bring people to Christ. It has been very rewarding watching my children grow in the ministry and having a personal love for God themselves. So many rewarding memories of when my children were in the sunshine band and purity class and now to see them all grown up and living productive lives and our ministry to God was a part of it all."

Over the years, Lady Matthews has been employed in the workforce for 27 years, mostly in childcare. Within the Church, Lady Matthews has served in the following capacities: Prayer Warrior, Choir President, Women's Department President, Primary age – Sunday School Teacher, Youth

20

Department President, District Youth Dept. - YPWW (Young People Willing Workers) President, Jurisdictional Superintendent Wives Circle, and currently serving in the role of Regional Chairperson for the Jurisdictional Supervisor.

In her spare time, Lady Matthews enjoys doing things such as: putting puzzles together, the type of puzzle with three to four thousand pieces, and making family collages, sewing, crafts, and jogging.

What have you learned as the Pastor's Wife that you wish you had have known before you stepped into the role?

"I have learned that it's not about the Pastor and me getting married and me having him all to myself. The children came, and the Church started growing. My husband, the Pastor, has always been a good provider and taken good care of the needs of our family. I learned to give myself in prayer and the "Word." Honestly, I really don't know how I would have made it this far had not God have been so good to us."

At the end of your life, on earth, how would you want people to remember you?

"I would like people to remember that I would think about people kindly in sending a greeting card, and people think, 'Wow, how did she know what I was going through?' I would want it remembered that I took the care and time to make those timely and empathetic connections; from a place of love." I would want it remembered that I'd been led by God to do this with people from all walks of life and hope that my kindness, over the years, was the definition of who I was."

21

Mother Matthews, please say something to all of those who will read this book. What would you want them to hear from you? Please, leave an encouraging word.

No, I never envisioned myself being married to a preacher; but I was blessed to have a woman in my life who was my Pastor's Wife. I watched her closely, she had a Spirit about her that drew people, and she knew how to encourage you. There was an anointing about her. Many of the sisters modeled after her.

"I would say you need to know who you are and be confident in your God that He has placed you in your marriage, and you are to be a prayer warrior. Being a prayer warrior is a must because when things aren't going your way, prayer and the "Word" will allow you to see yourself first AND THEN others. Being in the place of the Pastor's Wife is a place of Spiritual warfare, and it is best to remember that the warfare you will come up against is not about you.

"You must cover your husband, your love, your companion, your Pastor in prayer. You must know that the enemy consistently is setting traps, and there are many ways the enemy, in warfare, will come against you both.

"Know and remember that it is all about the ministry! This is how I survived many pitfalls. Another big word is 'obedient.' When we, the Pastor's Wife, are obedient to god, there's no good thing that God will withhold from you, His daughter. It was a lesson I had to learn. I learned much in my latter years. So much, I did not realize in my former years. I wouldn't take nothing for my journey now."

CHAPTER TWO

Lady Laura Richards/Colorado

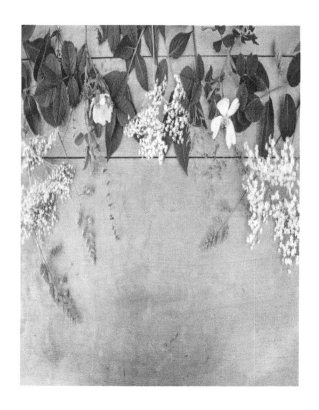

*M*y family was catholic. My family, as I remember it, did not show feelings very readily. Crying over something was not something we did in front of others. It was highly frowned upon, and even as a child, I knew this. It was my grandfather that I felt the most comfortable and could be myself with.

"I recall being at my grandmother's house. I was probably five or six years old. She had a big family Bible with the pictures in it. I saw a picture of "Jesus" on the cross, and I asked her who it was. She told me it was "Jesus." I felt like crying as I looked at this picture. 'How could people do this to Him?' I knew better than to cry, here and now, so I held it in. My Grandmother did not elaborate on who Jesus was and what had happened to Him.

"As I got older, I somehow felt that something else was out there. I had never felt comfortable in Church. These were my thoughts: 'The organist can't play. The man up front is doing these things with his hands....'

"There were so many things that contributed to my misunderstanding of so much at this point in my life!

"I felt my grandfather was the only somebody that loved me; my biological father had wandering hands. He was a happy drunk with beer and would turn violent when he'd had hard liquor! There was this time I remember when he hung me against the wall by the throat because he felt somebody's finger had been in the peanut butter; then there was the time he had tried to drown me when I was eight years old. I considered suicide at eight years old because of all that I was going through. Even presently, I am speaking with a counselor concerning these things.

"Years later, I married Joe, and it was a very abusive marriage. At this time, I did not know Jesus. I would lie to get out of the house, and those times I

I remember praying, 'Lord, I don't need a man in my life, but I sure would like to share it with somebody.

would sneak out, I would sometimes attend Church and an Al anon meeting specifically for survivors of an alcoholic family member. In my pain, I would take 'alcoholic shots' to go to sleep. I became pregnant with our son. I wanted my son to feel loved. I didn't want him to experience life as I had. I wanted my son to have that sense of belonging and security. Even though I was nauseous most of the time during my pregnancy, I loved being pregnant. Before my husband passed away, we went through a difficult divorce that involved a fierce custody battle for my son Ryan.

"Fast forward, I was now living for Jesus, and I had a very good Church home. I was plugged in there! I remember praying, 'Lord, I don't need a man in my life, but I sure would like to share it with somebody.' I had begun this college class, and in the winter of that year, I met Mark. This was back in the day when computers had floppy discs and mine had contracted a computer virus. Mark, a classmate, was being kind and trying to help me to fix the situation.

"Mark later drove me home. He did not come in. 'Mark, what are you doing on Sunday? We're having a Christmas program at Church?' He literally drove an hour to come to the Christmas Program. He was so touched by what he saw and heard that day, his eyes welling up with tears. He came by my apartment crying and gave his heart to the Lord. He was in Church every Sunday and Wednesday after that!

"We later were married. This marriage was a blessing. Our relationship was sweet! This man adored me, and I adored him too. We were serving the Lord together.

"Mark had accepted Jesus as His personal Lord and Savior and was loving Him with all he had. He simply had a hunger and thirst for righteousness! He was determined he was gonna serve, and he felt the leading of the Lord to serve to the best of his ability the senior Pastor of our Church. Mark had not been raised in the Church and did not know as much as some others, but he knew that God was calling him to serve, and God had given him this great big servant's heart. So, he went to the Pastor and told him that he felt God wanted him to help him; he desired to be the Pastor's armor-bearer."

You are reading the testimony of Lady Laura Richards. Her real-life testimony is so thought-provoking and intense at times, and I want us to see and hear her story from her own vantage point. Her story goes on…

> *Then there were headaches. He was having headaches. He had recovered from that "c" word years before he had met me, but when we went to check things out medically, the cancer had returned and this time it was in his brain. We were now a year and a half into our sweet marriage.*

"No way did I ever think I would be a minister's Wife. It never crossed my mind, but here I was. My husband was now the Assistant Pastor of the Church. They worked well together, my husband having such a humble heart, enjoying serving.

"Then there were headaches. He was having headaches. He had recovered from that "c" word years before he had met me, but when we went to check things out medically, the cancer had returned, and this time it was in his brain. We were now a year and a half into our sweet marriage.

> *Mark, was very devoted to "serving." There was the time where we had this weekend trip planned with the view of this beautiful lake. I was excited for this special time with he and I, THEN the phone rang! There was a need for him to go …the Pastor needed him to accompany him somewhere and yes, he went! I was mad! These ministers are at the Church's beck and call. Being the determined one that I am, I felt I was going to go anyway, and I did! I called a friend, and we went anyway and had a great time!*

"Treatments were begun immediately to attack the clusters of cancer in his brain. During all of this, my husband was witnessing to the doctors. There were some good reports that would come to us, and we'd have a time of winning the battle; but after a time, they again returned.

"Mark and I renewed our vows on Valentine's Day of that year. That same year Mark went to be with the Lord. We had been married for 7 ½ years. It was bittersweet. I was disappointed and happy. HE WAS HEALED just over in Heaven. It took me two years to realize that Mark's mission was over. It was very hard. This man was my soul mate; he was perfect for me! We walked together. Mark and I had something together that I had not had with anybody else. We even witnessed together. I just loved being with him.

"I was not doing well. Although I knew that Mark was now with the Lord, that he now had no more pain and suffering and that I had been blessed to be there 'til the very last moment yet I was having a very hard time. Finally, a friend and I took a cruise, and God used this cruise to bless my socks off, so to speak. God would talk with me on the deck of that ocean liner. I just had to be thankful for all the time God had given us to be together. It had been such a gift! I had to realize that Mark had completed his assignment for the Lord, and I was not yet done. God still had something for me to do on earth. I had to accept that, even though it hurt so bad. It has been a few years now, and I have not taken my wedding rings off; I just don't want to."

Lady Laura, we do extend to you our loving condolences and hugs. If we may go back a way before Pastor Mark's passing, would you mind sharing any challenges you may have faced as a Pastor's Wife?

"Mark was very devoted to "serving." There was the time where we had this weekend trip planned with the view of this beautiful lake. I was excited for this special time with he and I, THEN the phone rang! There was a need for him to go … the Pastor needed him to accompany him somewhere, and yes, he went! I was mad! These ministers are at the Church's beck and call. Being the determined one that I am, I felt I was going to go anyway, and I did! I called a friend, and we went anyway and had a great time!"

Would you mind sharing with us something else that you learned being a Pastor's Wife?

"Well, I learned to give of myself more. I helped in the kitchen and the nursery. We opened our home to foster children and such. Mark and I took on teaching Sunday School classes for the Youth. I was learning to be obedient to God with that. I was so blessed to serve the young people, submit to God, and to teach alongside my husband."

Lady Laura, tell us, what would you like to be remembered for at the end of your life?

"I want people to remember that I never quit. I want them to remember that if I failed, that I was humble enough to apologize and keep on going; because the only time you are a failure is when you quit!"

Would you mind speaking to that Pastor's/Minister's Wife who may have just had to say goodbye to their beloved husband? What would you say to them?

"Never lose hope. It won't happen overnight. As long as there is breath in your lungs, you have to keep running the race. You don't have to understand it all. There was peace when he was gone. He wasn't in pain anymore."

To those with a living spouse, Lady Laura says:

"Be where you need to be to appreciate the time you have with your husband. In retrospect, I was involved with other activities (they were good activities in my community, but I wish now that I had spent that time with my spouse then. Remember, what made you fall in love with him in the first place, and let him know what you loved.

"Lift him up, support him. He is gonna have a lot coming at him. This is a joint thing; you might have to carry a lot of the load at home. You may have to help him to balance the load of home and ministry. When he was gone all the time, I had to be supportive of that, but there was that time I missed him and told him so. Sometimes I put my foot down, and he knew he needed to be there for me.

"Schedule date nights, and don't let anything insignificant interfere with that. You have to 'TAKE CARE OF THE COUPLE.' Ask for one day (weekly)—some time for just you two.

A few of Lady Laura's FAVORITE THINGS:

FAVORITE SONG(S): *You Say* by Lauren Daigle, *It Is Well With My Soul* (I sang at home going)

FAVORITE COLOR (S): Hunter Green, Burgundy, and Emerald Green

FAVORITE PASTIMES: Motorcycle Riding, Reading the Bible in a Year, and Grandchildren

Lady Laura, our prayers are certainly with you as you continue this journey with Our Lord. May God's Grace and Peace be multiplied to you and yours! THANK YOU for sharing your testimony with us.

CHAPTER THREE

Lady Paula M. Brown/Florida

𝒲ell, it is my pleasure to introduce to some and present to others no other than **Pastor Paula M. Brown**. She is from the "sunshine" state. I met her and her husband, the senior Pastor when I lived in the state of New York. They are a very loving and anointed couple and pray Monday – Friday on their ministry's "Facebook" page, beginning at five – A.M. Central Standard Time.

These two Pastors pray corporately "Live" on Facebook. When I would be dressing for work, I would be listening to them taking turns fervently and faithfully praying in the background The Times of Refreshing Ministries of Florida, Inc. This author gives a shout-out to these prayer warriors, and I invite you to tune in and pray with them as well if you would like.

> *I learned all the ways to act Churchy but was never taught the real principles of what it meant to live holy. I will never forget that day! God had to take me from all that was familiar, family, and friends and put me in a place where I had to grow Spiritually and mentally. I went into the military...*

I must say that Pastor Paula made this interview so smooth. She is so good with the flow of her words, and I will print them from her own mouth, so to speak. Let us now get to know her, Pastor Paula M. Brown.

Hi there, Pastor Paula. Thank you so much for allowing me to introduce you to the people. We're just going to start at the beginning if you don't mind. Tell us how you came to know the lord and your experience with receiving the Holy Spirit.

"It's funny, I like to tell people that I got saved several times, but there came that time when I got saved for real. I was raised in the Church. I learned all the ways to act Churchy but was never taught the real principles of what it meant to live holy. I will never forget that day! God had to take me from all that was familiar, family, and friends. And He put me in a place where I had to grow Spiritually and mentally. I went into the military, and while stationed in GA, the time came when my unit had to go to war. I remember seeking out someone in my unit who I knew was in Church and serving God. I went to him and asked him to pray with me, and he just blew me off. He told me, "I don't have time right now." I was so hurt and offended. I did not let it stop me, though. I knew I needed peace, and the only way I was going to get it, was to get to God. So, I climbed in the back of my little two-door hatchback car; I got on my knees and prayed the best way I knew how. I did receive the peace I was looking for, but I was still going to war. Really, I was on my way to know Jesus.

"While in Saudi Arabia, approximately eight days in, there was a Church service going on (we were allowed to have fellowship over there, with limitations). I went to service that night, and I could feel the Lord moving all over me. I began singing the song *Be Grateful*, by Walter Hawkins, and something within me broke. I was never the same again. Shortly after that, I received the Holy Spirit (also, while in Saudi Arabia). Once again, we were in another service. It was one of those services where we tarried for the Holy Ghost. I wasn't going to leave that place until I received all that God had for me. God did a whole overhaul in me. I came back to the states another vessel, ready to be used by God."

No, I never envisioned that I would one day be a Pastor's Wife. It was not an office I desired. Over the years, I watched how first ladies would act or how they were treated. It was not attractive to me at all.

Now that's just beautiful. You began to chase after God. I love it! Did you ever imagine that you would be married to a Pastor one day, and the role in which you stand is what you may have thought it would be? Why or why not?

"No, I never envisioned that I would one day be a Pastor's Wife. It was not an office I desired. Over the years, I watched how first ladies would act or how they were

34

treated. It was not attractive to me at all. To me, they were constantly disrespected. I felt they did not have a voice. I always felt that people expected them to sit and look pretty—hair always laid out, hats, etc. Additionally, many of them were messy (behind the scenes). I was not that person. Anytime I would meet any of them, they were not all that cordial to me, and I really did not like that. Even when I became a Pastor's Wife, there were other Pastor wives I would reach out to, and many treated me as if I was beneath them. I never really connected with them on that level. I now understand why I couldn't connect with them. It was because of the mandate God placed on my life. My relationship, my desire to be in a relationship, had to be that of God and not man. I could not worry what one would think of me. God accepted me for who I am, and I needed to be content with that. Once I accepted who I was and stopped trying to get people to accept and validate me, I was able to really minister to others. I learned how to be open about my past, things that I've done and been through, which helped others get their deliverance. Too often, people are ashamed of their past and don't wish to share their past because of fear that someone will judge them. Me, I don't care. The past has passed, and no one can hold it against you. God doesn't even hold our past against us. Refer to Hebrews 10:17."

How did you meet your husband, the Pastor?

"Well, I got orders, and it wasn't until I was stationed in Germany that I met my wonderful husband. It was a setup from the very beginning. When I got there, I was held over at the reception center for 30 days. I had a daughter who was an EFMP family member, and I had to be located within 15 minutes of a major hospital, and where they were sending me was going to be well over an hour away. Again, this was another setup because I did not know what God had in store for me when I arrived at my permanent duty station.

35

"I stayed in the barracks until I was able to get on-post housing for my daughter and me. There was a Church, which was located right outside my window. One day, I was coming back from visiting a friend. As I opened my window, I heard someone yell, very loudly, "hallelujah"! It shook me to my core. I said to myself, "I've gotta go to that Church." This marked another transition in my life. That Sunday, I attended a service, but I did not see my husband in that service. Funny enough, he was putting his ex-Wife on a plane back to the states. One of the sisters had told me about a choir rehearsal they were having and invited me to it, and I did go that rehearsal, and there he was, on the keyboard, teaching choir rehearsal. I had no idea what God had in store for us. He asked for a volunteer to sing lead on a song, and no one raised their hand, so I volunteered, but because I was not a member, I could not sing. I got up and headed back to my barracks, and he literally stopped rehearsal and ran after me. It was amazing that he came. The room was full of women, but he came. Wow, he stopped everything just for me. He invited me to come out with the choir, for pizza, after rehearsal. I said yes, but later, changed my mind. The Pastor had come in that night and addressed some issues. There were some things that transpired that night during choir rehearsal, which made me indecisive about joining that particular ministry the following Sunday. Later that week, I attended a Bible study, and there he was again, but this time, he was teaching Bible study. I still love to hear him teach to this day. He is an awesome teacher, and he loves it. He was just a minister, but he wore several hats.

"Did I mention that he was raising his son and daughter? I was impressed, but it wasn't until I was at a point of decision-making in my life that God sent him by my place to check on me and minister to me. It was like we had known each other for many, many years. We clicked! My husband likes to say, "We fit like a glove." Before he left, he prayed with me, and to this day, we are still praying together. I remember how, while we were dating, we used to fall asleep on the phone while praying together. Our relationship started with prayer and was built through prayer."

36

How long have you served in the role of a First Lady? How long have you been married to your husband, the Pastor?

"I served in the role of a first Lady for approximately seventeen years prior to moving into the position of Pastor. We have been married for 28 years."

Yes, Ma'am, twenty-eight years! Congrats! God is good! What are the specific titles you have been associated with?

"In 1987, when we first started our ministry, I did carry the label "First Lady," and later, God transitioned me to serve in the capacity of a Pastor. I am the Pastor of the ministry, and my husband is Bishop/Senior Pastor. Actually, one must understand that when one is called to Pastor, the spouse is called to that same position. When married, God acknowledges them as "one." The problem is that the Church, as a whole, has brought separation by labeling a person "first Lady/man." It gives one authority over another, and that is something God never intended."

Would you mind sharing with us some of the challenges you have encountered during your time as a Pastor's Wife?

"Although there were many challenges, one of the major challenges I faced was having to deal with other women in the ministry. God's anointing on one's life is so attractive that I believe many have misplaced feelings. Unfortunately, many Pastors, who don't really have the heart of God, take advantage of a situation like this, and things happen that should not be mentioned amongst the Saints. When you really have an anointed Pastor, who loves the people and does not have a problem with taking time to minister one on one with people, some are led to establish false emotions and

37

misdirected feelings for their Pastor. This is something that could go either way, whether it be a man or a woman. At one point in our ministry, I believe every woman came up against me. I was so hurt and wanted to run. I did not want to run from God or my husband, but I did not want to be in that position. My husband came to a place that he told me if it would cost our relationship, then he would shut the ministry down. I endured. I made it through. I had to really learn what it meant to receive the garment of praise for the Spirit of heaviness. Refer to Isaiah 61:3. This scripture is how I make it through anything I encounter."

Yes, Ma'am, I appreciate you being honest. You explained the attractiveness of God's Anointing on one's life so well.

> *The most important thing that I could point out while on this journey is the fact that I am able to do it with someone who loves God just as much as I do.*

Please, also tell us of the joys you have had as you have ministered along with your Pastor and husband.

"The most important thing that I could point out while on this journey is the fact that I am able to do it with someone who loves God just as much as I do. He loves me greatly and shows it. We do everything together. We don't make a major move unless we are in agreement. After our youngest graduated from high school, God shifted our ministry and moved us to Florida. I tell people that God moved us here to give us rest. Although we are still Pastors, we have an awesome group of people that God has blessed to support us. If we must travel for ministry, many are free to travel with us, and if they are not able to travel with us, they provide ways for us and/or others to travel with us. Because we endured hardness, as a good soldier, the first eighteen years of our ministry, he has eased the load. God taught us to support each other, no matter what. Just as children tend to play the parents against one another, we realized that members of the body, at times, play those same games. The enemy figures, if he can tear down the leadership, he can destroy the Church. We stand united!"

Hallelujah! That part about agreeing, standing united, I thank God for your overcoming testimony, written here in MEET THE PASTOR'S WIFE, so many will be encouraged to continue standing lovingly beside their husband.

Pastor Paula, tell us the various places of service you have served in and around the Church congregation.

"I have done so much in ministry. Honestly, I don't know where to begin. I believe we can all say that we've been an usher before. Being an usher or singing in the choir is usually the first job one is appointed to or given. I believe it happens like this because when growing in Christ, we are trying to learn our identity, so we are taught to work. Do something.

"I have ushered, worked hospitality, choir, praise team, evangelist, Pastoral committee, fed the homeless, taught children's Church, adult teacher, choir president, etc. You name it! Once you become Pastors and are trying to build your ministry, you take on many roles. Sometimes, it is necessary until God sends you the people. He has to further your ministry."

What have you learned as the First Lady that you wish you had known before you stepped into the role?

"You may not believe this, but I am glad that I did not know what I was getting into before God called us to Pastor. I say this because had I listened to others or known what to expect, then I would have gone into this role with false expectations. God deals with everyone differently. We are all part of this body and have a role to play, which should be led by the Almighty. Something that worked for one may not work for another. You must seek God first. Refer to Matthew 6:33. I will say, however, know who you are in God. If you are married, you and your spouse need to provide a united front and never let anyone bad mouth your spouse. It causes a breakdown in your relationship, as well as the ministry."

Lady Paula, would you mind speaking about the calling to serve TOGETHER and a couple's 'Covenant Relationship."

"It always amazes me how God uses us. When God called us to start the ministry, He called US! I stress that because, as I stated before, God called us to be "one." As he was dealing with my husband, he was dealing with me as well. In order to serve in such a capacity, we believe husband and Wife must be on one accord, or it could wreck a marriage. As I stated earlier, my husband had declared to shut our ministry down for the sake of

> *Our congregation is very small but powerful. I am glad to say that God has given us a group who are hungry for His word.*

our relationship. Had he done this, I believe God would have honored this because he first established a covenant relationship through union/marriage. I knew I could not allow my husband to do something like that. He knew what God had called him to do. It was me that had not fully accepted what God was doing. In our ministry, I was so hurt, by the people, because I was the one who was doing everything for everybody. I was the hands-on person—serving, but my husband was the one getting all of the credit."

Talk to us about the congregation that you and your husband serve as Pastors, please:

"Our congregation is very small but powerful. I am glad to say that God has given us a group who are hungry for His word. It seems the more people there, the more problems the ministry has. I know that sounds crazy, but if you have ever served in ministry in any capacity, then you understand.

40

You have to know that you have been called, by God, to Pastor people. To Pastor means to serve, not command, or lord over God's people. I once read, "It is impossible to serve God, without serving one another. —Allistair Begg". Over the years, I have watched people leave our ministry and start their own because they did not like the way we handled things. Many did not like the patience we had with people or how we would not make people do things. My husband and I try and give people the same opportunity God gave us—to change. We realize that everyone has the ability to hear from God; however, it does not mean that everyone is going to do what He says. God gave us all choices. We are still required to do our part, whether our congregation is mega or small."

Amen. Amen! Well said! I thank God for the Blessed Ministry you all are doing there at the Times of Refreshing Ministries Inc. there in Florida. May God continue to do the 'Exceedingly, Abundantly, above all, in Jesus' name.

Pastor Paula, many will read this book, where you are being 'Introduced to some and presented to others.' What would you like to say to them?

"I believe we all have a story to tell, but my hope is that someone who reads this will be able to identify with their struggles and yet, not be afraid to allow God to use them. My desire is to make a difference in the body of Christ, in the Kingdom of God. "Our aim in serving God is to bring Him glory. Let's commit ourselves to making a difference in the Body of Christ with our gifts, abilities, and traits."—Author unknown.

If your congregation were to send you and your husband on an all-expense-paid vacation to anywhere, where would you want to go?

"We have traveled so many places, in our 28 years of marriage; I really don't have a place in mind. Back in the day, my heart's desire was to go to Hawaii, and that is a trip we were able to take for our 25th Anniversary. If I had to choose another place, I would choose China. I'd choose China because of my husband. This is a place he wishes to visit. He does so much for me, and it is so very rare that he thinks of himself or does anything for himself. He has always been so selfless, which taught me to be that way as well. I don't think I've ever been a selfish person, but I had always been so independent that I would never let anyone do anything for me. God had to break me of that, and I believe he used my husband to aid in that transition. In the early stages of our ministry, this question would not be on the table. Let someone send you on vacation. Not so! Trust me, I have learned through the years that God puts people in place to bless you. He has blessed us and created us to be a blessing."

Simply put, my heart's desire is to have an impact on the Kingdom of God. I want people to know me by the love that I show to others and know that I love God with all of my heart.

Yes, Maam, you just can't tell who has a burning desire to bless their Pastors in such a way. It is my prayer for you all that one day you'll make that vacation trip to China. From what I already know of you two, you deserve it!

At the end of your life on Earth, how would you want people to remember you?

"Simply put, my heart's desire is to have an impact on the Kingdom of God. I want people to know me by the love that I show to others and know that I love God with all of my heart."

42

A few of Pastor Paula's FAVORITE THINGS:

Do you have any extracurricular activities that you do outside of the Church scene? (Run a business – what type? Sewing, crafts, jogging, etc.)

"My husband and I walk together every day. Additionally, we love to go to the beach, even if we don't get in the water. It's beautiful as well as relaxing. We live in Florida. It's one of the vacation capitals of the world. There is so much to do, and we are always out and about doing something to relax us. All our children are grown and out of the house. We have our occasional visits from the grandchildren, which we absolutely love. I believe in having a life outside of ministry. Some have made Church their whole life and don't know how to live; therefore, they find themselves getting burnt out. God created this world for us to enjoy, and we do our best to enjoy it. We travel often and love it. My plan is to visit every state, at least once and go overseas, as much as possible."

FAVORITE COLOR(S):

Green, the color of nature. It is a color that is used to soothe and relax people, a color of newness and growth. I've liked this color my whole life before I even knew the meaning.

FAVORITE SONG (S):

"One of my favorite songs is *I'm Expecting Great Things* by Preashea Hilliard. I believe the title speaks for itself, and the other is a newer song called *Lord You are Good* by Todd Galbreath." Again, I believe the reason why is in the title. They are songs that minister to me personally. I remember when I was in the world, there were songs I used to listen to when I was going through a bad relationship, but the songs I listened too, only made me feel worse. I love how these are able to encourage my heart and lift my Spirit."

FAVORITE FLOWER:

"THE MORNING GLORY FLOWER blooms and dies within a single day. In the Victorian meaning of flowers, morning glory flowers signify love and affection. They also represent the month of September and 11th wedding anniversaries."

FAVORITE SCRIPTURE: (why does this one stand out to you?)

"I have so many scriptures that minister to me, and I love, but the one that has carried me through so much is Isaiah 61:3 to appoint unto them that mourn in Zion, to give unto them beauty for ashes, the oil of joy for mourning, the garment of praise for the Spirit of heaviness; that they might be called the trees of righteousness, the planting of the Lord, that he might be glorified."

Special thanks to Pastor Paula! These "LADIES" have dug deep within their hearts to be transparent with us and to leave Holy Spirit-inspired encouragement with every reader. They are: *"Overcoming by their testimony and the Blood of the Lamb..."* (Rev. 12:11 paraphrase KJV).

Times of Refreshing Ministries of Florida, Inc. (Pastors Robert & Paula Brown)

5650 Wayside Drive

Sanford, Florida 32771

EIGHT BOOKS FOR PASTOR'S WIVES THAT'LL ENCOURAGE YOU

FOR MINISTRY LIFE

From the Bubbling Brook Blog

- SACRED PRIVILEGE by Kay Warren

- THE CHURCH PLANTING WIFE by Christine Hoover

- THE PASTOR'S WIFE: STRENGTHENED BY GRACE FOR A LIFE OF LOVE by Gloria Furman

- LEADING AND LOVING IT by Lori Wilhite and Brandi Wilson

- ZEAL WITHOUT BURNOUT by Christopher Ash

- ORDERING YOUR PRIVATE WORLD by Gordon MacDonald

- SHE CAN'T EVEN PLAY THE PIANO by various ministry wives, a compilation of stories

- HIGH CALL, HIGH PRIVILEGE by Gail McDonald

CHAPTER FOUR

Lady Yolanda Ferguson/Arkansas

Such a blessed opportunity to meet **Lady Yolanda Ferguson**. Meeting and interacting with her was a pleasant experience; she is a woman who is beautiful on the inside as well as out, and when she speaks, you hear God's Word and a 'Spirit of Wisdom' in her conversation. Lady Yolanda had much to share in the hopes that her transparency would help any other woman that would, unfortunately, be found in her similar experience of the past. This is a "Lady" indeed. She has walked the *Frontier of Forgiveness* and has held onto *God's Unchanging Hand.*

Many relationships have begun with the Lord. Vows were made with pure and Holy intentions, and a commitment was made before witnesses. We have all lived long enough to know, and to understand, that for whatever reason, even after all of this, some have stepped away from their marital commitment, some have not kept their vows to God or their spouse. Thankfully, this has not been and is not the case of all Pastoral marriages, but for the sake of "truth," we cannot act as if it has not ever happened.

I am introducing and presenting the testimony and true-to-life account of Lady Yolanda Ferguson.

She found herself in a situation that she never expected or wanted. The "Hallelujah!" part of this testimony is that years after all of this occurred, Lady Ferguson yet loves and lives for the Lord! She yet is 'Running for Jesus,' and her past "Mess is now her Message!"

I, the author, wanted to represent every Pastor's Wife's personal situation possible because somebody needs the encouragement, the inspiration, and even hope for a way of escape! Some 'Woman of God,' some Pastor's Wife, is going through this or similar. Maybe it is not you, but if the

48

truth is told, some Pastor's Wife is suffering behind closed doors; and we dare not simply turn our heads!

Some First Lady, somewhere, feels trapped and hurt. Some 'Woman of God' is continually being abused by a man who wears a clergy collar and is assigned to the flock of God. There is a First Lady who feels alone in the situation. Therefore, Lady Yolanda chose to be transparent about her own past circumstance, as she was married to a Pastor years ago. For this chapter, there is a pseudo (fake) name and location, and some details have been changed to protect the privacy of all who may have been involved in all that happened in this real-life account.

DISCLAIMER: I AM NOT A LICENSED PSYCHOLOGIST OR COUNSELOR; CERTAINLY, THERE ARE CHRISTIAN COUNSELORS AVAILABLE IN MANY AREAS; AND IN THE MEANTIME, PRAYER DOES CHANGE THINGS: "MANY ARE THE AFFLICTIONS OF THE RIGHTEOUS, BUT THE LORD DELIVERS HIM OUT OF THEM ALL" (PSALM 34:19 KJV).

Lady Yolanda begins:

"I was actually married to my husband (the Pastor) for 18 years. He was a young minister and evangelist when I met him. He is the one who introduced me to Christ. I am saved today because of his evangelistic witness. You see, I grew up Catholic, and the whole concept of living Holy was new to

> *It was here at this Church musical that I met the young man (serving as a minister in his Church at the time), who would later become my husband and Pastor.*

me, but I was open to learning about it once I heard it.

"Let me back up some and start from the beginning. I spent a lot of my time at the club. A friend and I, as usual, were headed to the club that night. She was a Church goer but was not living for the Lord at that time. They were having a musical at a local Church, and she was on the program to sing. My friend said, 'We'll run by the Church, I will sing, and

49

then we'll go on to the club." It was here at this Church musical that I met the young man (serving as a minister in his Church at the time), who would later become my husband and Pastor.

"He slipped me a piece of paper with his name and number on it. We began to get to know each other, and it was his evangelistic witness that introduced me to the saving grace of Jesus Christ. From my heart, I accepted Jesus into my life. It was not long after this that I was in my bedroom, kneeling beside my bed when I received the 'Baptism of the Holy Spirit with the evidence of speaking in tongues." Lady Yolanda says."

Lady Yolanda tells us a little more about her background:

"You know, being that I was raised catholic, I did not know much if anything about living a Holy life for the Lord; however, at the age of approximately twelve, I had this feeling that I would one day be a preacher's Wife. I know now that God was dealing with me, but then, it was just an impression I had felt, and I just knew that it was to happen one day. You see, I came to find out that my mother had tried to abort me three times. It is a miracle I was born and alive now to give any testimony of God's goodness. Just learning all of this let me know that God had and has a purpose for me. Therefore Jeremiah 29:11 is so dear to me. In all I had and would go through, God still had and has a Divine plan for my life. "For I know the plans I have for you, declares the LORD, plans to prosper you and not to harm you, plans to give you hope and a future." Over the years, God has graced me to lead others in my family to Him, such as my mom, dad, brother, and other family members. I thank the Lord because I feel very strongly about home ministry! What good is it if I can reach the world and my own family does not see God in me?" Lady Yolanda declares.

And so, you got married.

"Yes, as we continued to get to know each other, he told me that he had gone on a three-day fast and that the Lord had told him that I was to be his Wife. I was young in the faith, had big respect of him; (after all, he had led me to Christ and was mentoring me in certain ways, as well), and so I believed he had heard God; regarding marriage for us.

"We got married in 1985. We had dated about a year in a half, at the point of our marrying. I was in my early twenties then. It wasn't long before he became a Pastor and I the First Lady. I faced many challenges, more than I could have ever

> *There were jealous women, cunning women, around me; they wanted to be in my position – I still had to love and minister to them and I did.*

imagined. There were so many people in the Church that I met that did not understand the walk of a minister's Wife. That position is pure ministry! Let's see, (as she reflected): There were jealous women, cunning women, around me; they wanted to be in my position – I still had to love and minister to them, and I did.

"Basically, I was raising our child alone because my Pastor husband was also a traveling evangelist and was away much of the time. It was my child and me, and we basically saw my husband and Pastor about twice a month.

> *To add to all of this, senior ranking preachers (Bishops included) were hitting on me (making sexual advances). God had given me how to put them in place politely. I loved my husband, and more than that, I loved the Lord from my heart!*

"We are speaking of CHALLENGES. Right? To add to all of this, senior ranking preachers (Bishops included) were hitting on me (making sexual advances). God had given me how to put them in place politely. I loved my husband, and more than that, I loved the Lord from my heart!"

51

She continues.

"Meanwhile, I enjoy ministering, and I did so. God had gifted me. He had given me a great rapport with the people of the Church. Many of the women there would seek out my confidential counsel. God used me to minister to them. He saw this (my husband and Pastor) and was jealous of this! He would confront me and accuse me of trying to Pastor his Church. In his angry outbursts, he demanded that I stop interacting with those who sought to talk to and desire Christian counsel from me.

"I learned that my husband, Pastor, was carnal-minded! The man I loved and married, evangelizing soul that he was, had a form of godliness but denied the power thereof.' Refer to 2 Timothy 3:5-7 (KJV), "Having a form of godliness, but denying the power thereof: from such turn away...ever learning, and never able to come to the knowledge of the truth."

"He began to have affairs with other women; there were three adulterous affairs that I know of for sure that happened DURING OUR MARRIAGE. I also know that on

> *He began to have affairs with other women; there were three adulterous affairs that I know of for sure that happened DURING OUR MARRIAGE.*

at least one occasion, he impregnated a woman. Yes, all of this and more was at some point during the 18 years that I was married to him. I later found out that the men in his family, his father (an overseer in another denomination), his brothers, and more are also known womanizers in and about the Church congregation, having problems with sexual sin.

"In my heart, I was determined to make it work. I loved my husband and enjoyed ministry for the Lord; as a First Lady, these shoes were high-heeled (so to speak), but I felt I was graced to stand tall in them. I loved the people, and the people loved me. I wanted my marriage to work. It turns out that my now ex-husband, my now ex-Pastor, had never been fully delivered from sin. He needed deliverance! The truth is, he was plagued with generational curses, sexual sin in his life, and he was angry. He had an anger problem, and I suffered from his verbal abuse often!"

So, Lady Yolanda, you were greatly involved in ministry even while all of these "challenges" were going on?

"I honestly took my role as Pastor's Wife, teacher, counselor, and doing ministry at conferences, seriously. I have a calling on my life to do this, and I was working for the Lord as diligently as I could. I mean, I had to, my husband was gone most of the time, and he would leave me to teach Sunday School or Bible Study. In the beginning, he and I would travel to his speaking engagements together; but later, as he would get involved with other women, this would stop. I, too, had speaking engagements. I was invited to be a conference speaker ministering, in and around our geographical region, as well, and so we were a busy couple.

"There were times he would literally take to our Church pulpit and preach about me and to me in a negative way. What I mean by this is that whatever it seemed we were going through at home that he was irritated with me about, it would become the preached message once we got to Church. For instance, that scripture about "Wives obey your husbands" (Ephesians 5:22-33 KJV). He would wear that scripture out. He would not call my name, but many knew he was directing the message at and to me. There was a passive message hidden within the message. Little by little, I realized that it was not God's design, not His will, that Church be the place for people, even the First Lady, to sit and be abused.

"You're sitting there in your chair, all dressed up, some women looking at you with jealousy and envy of your position. They don't even know what this position entails; they don't realize nor care

53

what I am going through. You're sitting there making every attempt to hold in the tears 'til you can get somewhere safe to let it all out.

"Even still, he, as the Pastor of this congregation and I, as the Pastor's Wife, continued to go through the motions. The Church had been at a membership of 289 when we had first begun there, and in a year's, time had grown to over 1300."

> *You're sitting there in your chair; all dressed up, some women looking at you with jealousy and envy of your position. They don't even know what this position entails; they don't realize nor care what I am going through. You're sitting there making every attempt to hold in the tears 'til you can get somewhere safe to let it all out.'*

Tell me again how your jail ministry got started:

"Well, I mentioned before that he had an anger problem! He had not acknowledged this. He was not seeking out any help for this, and verbal abuse toward me began to escalate.

"We had come home one day, dressed in our Church best; he was upset with me about people coming to me, talking with me, and in his rage, he threw a glass of cranberry juice in my face. Again, he had an anger problem, and I was the prime one he would take his anger out on! Because of what he had done, and WITH **MY SAFETY IN MIND, I CALLED THE POLICE**. When the police came, they saw my Saintly-looking husband, dressed in his Pastoral suit and all, and believed his lie over the explanation I had given; never mind that I was the one who had called 911. **THEY TOOK ME TO JAIL**. I ended up staying three days. The Church congregation did not know. Who could I call? My husband, the Pastor most would trust, had been the one who had made my new JAIL MINISTRY TIME POSSIBLE!

"I called my dutiful, loving, and prayer warring assistant. She had seen and understood, and she had been an interceding confidant about the things my husband and I were going through. She had not

54

been an unwise blabbermouth, but she did tell her husband, who was one of the deacons (trustees) of the Church congregation, that I was in jail and why. She came and got me. I arrived home, and my husband, the Pastor, just said, 'I hope you learned something.'

"You asked about **'JAIL MINISTRY' and jail ministry it was.** Those three days got used and turned around for gospel good! God got the glory! I had the greatest opportunity to minister to those ladies in there with me, and (by God's grace), souls were saved in there! Just like that, God took what satan meant for harm and turned it around for good. Refer to Genesis 50:20 (KJV). I reflected on the Apostle Paul and how he had brought God's praises to the prison! Refer to Acts 16:16-40 (KJV.) Hallelujah!

"The next day, I was due to be at a conference away, and this was the International COGIC WOMEN'S CONFERENCE to be held out of state. Without missing a beat, my adjutant and I packed up and headed out the next day for the conference. Who would've known that I had just been released from a three-day jail stay!

"My marriage was on the rocks, and so was my husband's Pastoral position here at this Church. As word reached the Church's officials as to what had been going on, we were put out of the Church congregation. My husband was no longer the Pastor there, and I was no longer the First Lady.

"To this day, my ex-husband and Pastor continues to preach on the evangelistic field. At the point of this writing, he has been married at least three times. In recent years, a Pastor contacted me regarding my ex-husband, my ex-Pastor. It turns out that my ex, who had been a trusted evangelist preaching revivals and a trusted friend, had run off with this Pastor's Wife! He had been secretly (adulterously) dating this First Lady, and (now), they were planning to be married. This Pastor had located me because they wanted custody of his child, and he had wanted to know if this man could be a

55

trusted individual around his son or daughter. This man had trusted my ex as a Pastor and friend and was deeply hurt by all of this. I have just heard recently that this Pastor passed away. I wonder, not sure, but I wonder if he died of a broken heart."

Lady Ferguson, speaking of children, what about your own?

"Throughout the years since our child has gone through post-traumatic situations that stem from what we all went through with his father; praise God, our son has broken the sexual generational curse that my ex-husband was so bound up in. But up until this day, our child is in a struggle with anger issues; he also struggles with nicotine and alcohol issues. For these situations, thank you for your prayers."

I am sorry you and your family experienced all of this, and my prayers certainly for your son – salvation and the healing of his heart.

Would you fill us in? Since your divorce, what is your situation now? Have you moved on?

"Over the years, God has graced me to lead others in my family to Him, such as my mom, dad, brother, and other family members. My mother died of cancer a few years ago, but before she did, she accepted Jesus into her life. Hallelujah! I thank the Lord because I feel very strongly about home ministry! What good is it if I can reach the world, but my own family does not see God in me? I am currently enjoying the ministry of grand parenting! I am loving on them and pouring into them God's Word! I am in a beautiful Church fellowship now, and I have a Pastor that loves God in its purest form. I am faithful in attendance there! So many of the people I once served at the Church where I was a Pastor's Wife yet love and respect me, and I am thankful for that.

56

"Yes, I would marry again, and if it were God's will, I would marry a preaching Man of God, again as well; As a matter of fact, if it were God's will, I would even marry a man called to Pastor if he were, in fact, God-fearing and Holy Spirit-filled. IF THAT WERE GOD'S WILL FOR ME! As I mentioned before, I love people, and I love ministry. I was young and very young in the faith, and I just got joined up to the wrong soul."

Lady Yolanda, what would you say to a woman presently going through this or similar situations? How would you advise them?

"I would pray with her, walk her through it. If I knew she was going through this or similar, I would be her 'Ride 'n Die.' – so to speak. I would be the person to her that I felt I needed when I had gone through that. There is power and strength in groups. I would advise that she would find somebody to help walk her through it. (SPEAKING TO THE PASTOR'S WIFE) *"Those are some very **high-heeled shoes (symbolically)**, and every woman can't walk in them; as you go through various things, you'll need somebody. You mustn't try to do it alone; some things can cause you to lose your mind if you don't do things in God's way!* WE ALL NEED CHRIST, BUT I AM SPEAKING ON THE FLESH 'N BLOOD SIDE OF THINGS. Make sure your adjutant is Holy Spirit-filled and that she is truly for you. Make sure you can trust her, that she is fervently praying for you. ***You must pray about who is to walk with you. You can't take everybody with you. A special grace is needed to walk with and minister to the FIRST LADY!"***

CHAPTER FIVE

Lady Suzette Wright/Missouri

*f*avorite Scripture: Romans 8:35-39: "I'll let nothing separate me from the love of God...."

Lady Suzette Wright of Kansas City, Missouri, you could say, was born into the Church scene. She was a PK, also known as a Pastor's (Preacher's) kid. With a love for going to Church, a younger Suzette accepted Jesus Christ to be her precious Lord and Savior at the tender age of 17. She says: "I received the Holy Spirit in a revival shortly afterward." See Acts 1:8 (KJV).

"While living in Reno, Nevada, I was invited to attend a revival by a friend. It was after service that this friend introduced me to the invited guest speaker of this revival. My friend was thinking that we would make a good couple. Now I thought my well-meaning friend was wrong because there were no fireworks (between us) whatsoever." Lady Suzette says, "I wasn't interested in this full-time evangelist, and neither was he interested in me."

It turns out that this young man (as they say) was "On fire for the Lord" and praying for a Godly spouse, but their interaction to this point was seeming to go nowhere; they didn't

> *My friend was thinking that we would make a good couple. "Now I thought my well-meaning friend was wrong because there were no fireworks (between us) whatsoever." Lady Suzette says, "I wasn't interested in this full-time evangelist, and neither was he interested in me.*

like the other. Neither had any idea that it would not be long before they indeed would be together as a couple who would later be married. Their matchmaking friend continued with her quest and had them both to dinner one night. Lady Suzette found this gentleman to be humorous; apparently, he had all at the dinner party laughing out loud! She says that she and her husband, the Pastor, don't even realize exactly how it happened to this very day, but by the end of that dinner party, as they all walked to their cars, they were holding hands. Lady Suzette further adds, "I feel like that's when the Lord joined us together."

That young full-time evangelist has been a full-time Pastor for years now, and Lady Suzette has been by his side. She has served as the Pastor's Wife since 1971 – at the point of this writing, 50 years. When asked, did you have any idea of what being the Wife of the Pastor would entail, she says: "No, I had no idea as to what the role of a First Lady was. First, I felt lost and all alone. The people were friendly to my husband and ignored me as a First Lady. Sometimes there was jealousy shown toward me as the First Lady." First Lady Suzette continues, "The people expected too much of me as a First Lady. The members (of our Church congregation) would call the house and ask to speak to the Pastor and would not (even) ask how I was doing." This woman of God continues to reflect and say: "Many times the women will do things to try to entice my husband."

I, the author, know this beautiful Wife of the Pastor personally, and over the years I have known her, she in no way walks around with her head down in gloom. She is joyful and

> *"Many times, the women will do things to try to entice my husband."*

walks around fulfilling purpose with her every step. She certainly is a woman of wisdom!

> *There were some members who would do special things for us. One of the members sponsored a special day for me, (Queen for a Day).*

I asked her about the joys and blessings of being the Pastor's Wife, and she adds:

"Later in life, I began to enjoy and experience some good times. One Church member of our congregation gave my husband and me a free trip to Australia and the Bahamas. We were given several trips to Hawaii, and these were all-expense paid. Some members would do special things for us. One of the members sponsored a special day for me (Queen for a Day). They rolled out a red carpet decorated with money, a decorated chair with flowers, and other décor. Four members went together and made the expensive purchase of a beautiful crystal chandelier."

Lady Suzette is now a very seasoned "Mother in Zion," as many Churches respectfully label a woman who has served for years and is adored and respected for her long-time service in the Lord. She has served in many roles and has worn many proverbial hats, both inside and outside of the Church walls: She has read for elementary-aged students, cared for the elderly, been a wedding coordinator, and has done so free of charge. Mother Suzette's service within her place as the Pastor's Wife continues. She has done jail ministry for 35 years and lovingly administered 'Final Wishes' – helping others list and record all pertinent information needed in the case of a person's death and the putting together of all business required in that case. Within the Church walls, Mother Suzette has been president of the usher board, purity class (ages 12 – 17), hospitality committee, Young Women's Christian Council, Sunshine Band (ages 2 – 12), Mother's Board, Sunday School Secretary, and service in the Sunday School across the board, Chairperson of the benevolence committee, Seminar presenter for both the single and married couples, crafting and decorating. She is one of God's greatest because she is a faithful servant!

[NICHELLE'S NOTE – 4] *The above is quite a list of services and is an example of the extensive workload in and around our Church congregations that many of these Pastors' Wives take on. Regardless of the stereotype(s), Pastors' wives are more than pretty faces.*

I wish I had known the role of the Pastor's Wife. We need to seek the Lord about our role as the First Lady. As the 'Woman of God' married to the 'Man of God', we also have a ministry. God gives us a work to do as we work along by our husband's side. I would like to encourage all First Ladies to seek advice from an experienced Pastor's Wife who has a Godly reputation. Take some Bible study courses. Go to Bible college if you can. Be faithful to prayer. Stay as close to your husband as possible, love him and pray for him. You are his help mate. PLEASE DON'T BE JEALOUS! Be strong and know that you are somebody in the Lord.

Mother Suzette understood the purpose of this book and this author's desire to have each Pastor's Wife's input to be an encouragement to another, and these are words she has given for that purpose.

"I wish I had known the role of the Pastor's Wife. We need to seek the Lord about our role as the First Lady. As the 'Woman of God' married to the 'Man of God', we also have a ministry. God gives us a work to do as we work along by our husband's side. I would like to encourage all First Ladies to seek advice from an experienced Pastor's Wife who has a Godly reputation. Take some Bible study courses. Go to Bible College if you can. Be faithful to prayer. Stay as close to your husband as possible, love him and pray for him. You are his help mate. PLEASE DON'T BE JEALOUS! Be strong and know that you are somebody in the Lord."

THIS IS A DECLARATION TO LIVE BY EVERY DAY

I declare I will live victoriously

I was created in the image of God

I have the DNA of a winner

I am wearing a crown of favor

Royal blood flows through my veins

I will live with purpose, passion, and praise, knowing that I was destined to live in victory

THIS IS MY DECLARATION in Jesus' name

CHAPTER SIX

Lady Danielle Neary/New York

_𝒪_t is my pleasure to introduce to the reader our next Pastor's Wife, **Lady Danielle Neary.** I must let you know that I greatly admire this young "Lady." In the state of New York (NNY), my family has had both the privilege and honor of fellowshipping in the same Church congregation with their family years ago! Knowing her family has been a joy! We will all be blessed as we hear her own personal testimony. So now,

"I INTRODUCE TO SOME AND PRESENT TO OTHERS: PASTOR DANIELLE NEARY.

So, Pastor Danielle, I understand that you are always a "Lady," but you work beside your husband as a Pastor. Please tell us about your activities outside of the four walls of the Church. How do you busy yourself?

*My husband, and Pastor, Michael, have **eight children** (**seven boys and one girl**); so, a lot of my time is spent being a 'HOMESCHOOLING MOM,' which is my other favorite role. I also really enjoy personal development and I am working towards becoming a Christian Life Coach.*

"My husband, and Pastor, Michael, have eight children (seven boys and one girl); so, a lot of my time is spent being a 'HOMESCHOOLING MOM,' which is my other favorite role. I also really enjoy personal development, and I am working towards becoming a Christian Life Coach."

Amen! That is a beautiful life but also a very busy one. It would seem. Please, go on.

"It can be a challenge to balance ministry with family life, but I have learned that being intentional with my time has really helped. Our children are Michael, Jr. 18, Cameron 17, Christian 14, Josiah 10, Jesse 8, Titus 7, Shiloh 5, and Gracelyn 3."

What a beautiful family you have been blessed with, and I love their names. I was there several times when at least three of these dear children was being dedicated to the Lord. I remember being excited for you when little Gracelyn was born. That cute little girl has a house full of

> *It can be a challenge to balance ministry with family life, but I have learned that being intentional with my time has really helped. Our children are Michael, Jr. 18, Cameron 17, Christian 14, Josiah 10, Jesse 8, Titus 7, Shiloh 5, and Gracelyn 3.*

bodyguards! It is hard for me to believe that she is already three years.

And your decision to homeschool, please tell us a little about that part of your journey.

"We began our homeschool journey 13 years ago when our oldest son was a second-grader at the local public school. A few weeks into the year, we realized that he was struggling to retain the information taught and could possibly benefit from the one-on-one education that homeschooling provides. What I learned from that year is still my driving force and why I continue to homeschool today! It helped to form the bond between Michael, Jr., and me, as well as and continues to build my own character day after day.

"After that first year, I asked my husband to pray about the rest of the children's homeschooling, as well. It was toward the end of the summer, and he agreed. We would home school them all. Since we began, some of our children have again returned to the public school, as they have gotten older to participate in the sports programs.

"This year, I will be homeschooling four of our children in Pre-School, Kindergarten, Second and Third grades."

WOW, I can just imagine how busy you will be. You are so dedicated, you and your hubby. You have been raising eight children and doing ministry, and it is amazing the grace God has given you.

Now, as I mentioned before, you are a mother of eight (such a blessing), and for years I remember you were a "Boy Mom." I remember hearing your ministering husband speak of his baseball team, and I even had the opportunity to watch some of your "Little Men" play ball, as well. I believe our whole community in Small Town, North Country (Upstate New York) rejoiced when we heard of your little girl arriving. Tell us about it, please.

"Gracelyn is the only girl out of our children, and trust me when I tell you, I was thrilled! After being a "Boy Mom" for fourteen years, I was ready and excited for sparkles and bows. Gracelyn has confidence like no other, which I believe is because she is so adored by us all."

Now, I know there are other mothers of infants and school-aged children who are doing their prayerful best to manage ministry, marriage, and family by God's grace. I have watched you before and can see that God has given you and your spouse "grace" for it all.

Pastor Danielle, please share some of what you do in managing a loving and God-fearing home for your big and beautiful family.

"I utilize my time in the mornings before my children wake up as well as in the evenings after they are in bed. That is when I study the Word of God.

> *I utilize my time in the mornings before my children wake up as well as in the evenings after they are in bed. That is when I study the Word of God.*

"I start my mornings off with prayer and journaling. I typically write a scripture verse that jumps out to me while reading; then I write out some declarations that align with God's Word, and I finish by writing out three things I am thankful for. This sets the tone for my entire day and brings me into a heart of gratitude.

"I often get ministry-related work done after I spend time with the Lord or in the evenings. Michael and I are a team, and we try to work together as much as possible when the other has ministry-related work that needs to be done, whether it be a sermon or projects we are working on.

"We really enjoy the relational aspect of ministry and like to involve our entire family in that which benefits all of us. We do this by inviting families over to share a meal with *us.*

At this point in the interview, I just must chime in and say that I am thankful that my family was blessed to have been one of those families invited over to their home for a meal. It was actually more than that, and it was a great festive fellowship. The Neary's did not have as big of responsibility in ministry as they do now (they were not yet Pastors, but I have not ever known them when they were not busy; yet they had for me and mine, an open home and open heart; and apparently even with the Pastoral responsibility hospitality is still in their heart).

> *Michael and I are a team, and we try to work together as much as possible when the other has ministry-related work that needs to be done, whether it be a sermon or projects we are working on.*

"Show hospitality to one another without grumbling"

(1 Peter 4:9 ESV).

I believe Lady Danielle was expecting baby number six, and she was very close to delivery time! Yet she cooked us and others a delicious meal and was joyful throughout. Meanwhile, there was

69

an obstacle course-like activity outside that Michael was entertaining all our children with and more. This was a memorable Sunday evening!

"Having a large family, I had to figure how to stay organized, out of necessity! My planner is always close to me, and I write everything down. I like to take a few minutes at the end of the night to plan the next day and the goals of that day and to go over any scheduled events we may have.

"To stay connected, Michael and I enjoy going on dates together, and we love that our older children are willing to spend the evening with their siblings so we can make that happen. We also try to have one day within each week where we have no scheduled plans, and the family just hangs around the house playing baseball outside, playing board games, or doing puzzles. We like this time to slow down a little and regroup just to be with each other.

Simply amazing! I am excited about the journey God has you on! Tell us, how did you come to know Jesus and receive the baptism in the Holy Spirit?

"I came to know Jesus when I was around 12 years old; through my summers spent attending an all-girls Christian camp. I walked away from the Lord during my teenage years and then returned and completely surrendered my life at age 22. I received the Holy Spirit a year or two afterward, while alone and in my prayer time."

And your husband – Pastor Neary, how did you and he come to meet?

"We love to share our story, the story of how we met because we believe it is such a redemption story of God's grace and what He can do with two broken people. Michael and I met in a nightclub in downtown Buffalo, NY. Neither one of us was serving the Lord at that time.

"Michael was not Pastoring or ministering before we had met. He did not know the Lord or the plan God had for his life at that time. Soon after we met, a friend started sharing with him who Jesus was, and he surrendered his life to the Lord. His life started to change in so many ways completely, and all for the better.

Pastor Danielle, did you ever envision that you'd be married to a minister/Pastor one day? Did it ever come to mind?

"When I was younger, I never thought I would be a Pastor's Wife or a Pastor myself; however, once my husband and I began serving the Lord, we both recognized something was different, and we knew that we would have some role in ministry. Ministry is what I thought it would be and more!

"As it turns out, I served as a Pastor's Wife for three years and recently moved into the new role of co-Pastoring alongside Michael. Michael became a staff Pastor soon after receiving his licensing at the Church we attended and were married in. He then went on to Pastor a Church as the lead Pastor for three years which was a wonderful experience for both of us and taught us many things. We took some time out of ministry before entering back into the role recently, where we both were hired on as Pastors in our current positions."

Sweet! Congratulations on the promotion. May many souls be saved and shepherded through your ministry to others. When we see one of you, there is the other. You are a team!

Speak to us about challenges. Have there been any challenges?

I definitely have encountered some challenges, especially understanding that Church life is something that is ever-changing. People come and go, and I have to know that when this happens that it isn't personal.

What about the joys of ministry?

"The biggest joys I have experienced is when I watch Michael being the person that God created him to be and flourishing in ministry. I also would say the same about myself in the role that I am in. When you are doing what God made you for, you have such peace and understanding of the bigger picture even through the hard times. We have been married now, 14 years, and are blessed in what God is now doing!"

Pastor Danielle, you have made it one of your goals to become a Christian life coach. Tell us about this, please.

"One of the biggest reasons I wanted to become a Certified Christian Life Coach is to help moms find a love of mothering without feeling constantly overwhelmed. I would really like to be a part of helping these to learn how to live out the 'Abundant' life that God has promised us!

"I want women to know that they have a purpose and can dream. I want to empower them to reach their dreams and find deep fulfillment in living the lives God created explicitly for them to live!"

72

May God bless you to inspire mega many as you coach many to that 'abundant life' that Christ offers! May God bless you in your endeavors!

We have just a few more questions for the reader to get to know you a little better. At the end of your life, on earth, how would you want people to remember you?

"At the end of my life, I want people to look at my life and be able to say that I carried the peace of God and influenced the people and situations around me. I want to be remembered as a world-changer who walked by faith while boldly motivating others to take action and be all that God created them to be. I want to be known as a risk-taker and someone that was sold out for Jesus."

What have you learned as you work beside your husband that you wish you had known before you stepped into this current role of ministry?

"I have learned that even when it doesn't seem like what we are doing is making a difference, it really is making a difference in the 'Kingdom of God.'"

"I also wish that I had known that the ministry God had for our family might have looked different than other families in ministry. I wish I had known that it is 'OK' for our family just to be who we are. I know now that we can be ourselves in Christ!"

FAVORITE SONG(S):

As the Deer and *It Is Well With My Soul*

FAVORITE SCRIPTURE:

> *I wish I had known that it is 'OK' for our family to just be who we are. I know now that we can be ourselves in Christ!*

"My favorite scripture is Luke 4:18, which says, "The Spirit of the Lord is upon me, because he hath anointed me to preach the gospel to the poor; he hath sent me to heal the brokenhearted, to preach deliverance to the captives, and recovering of sight to the blind, to set at liberty them that are bruised..."

I like this verse because it gets me excited about acting on it when it comes to our faith to share the Gospel; and allowing God to use us in whatever capacity He sees fit.

If your Church congregation were to send you and your husband on an all-expense-paid vacation to anywhere, where would you choose to go?

"I would like to go to the "Ocean" and relax near the water. Michael would probably enjoy a cabin in the woods, near a really great fishing spot."

Why did you choose the 'sunflower' to represent you?

The 'Sunflower' represents unwavering faith and I believe that is what my journey and walk with Christ are, in so many ways.

"The 'Sunflower' represents unwavering faith, and I believe that is what my journey and walk with Christ are, in so many ways."

'Woman of god,' thank you for sharing with us, loving Jesus, your husband, children, and those souls you lovingly serve! God will reward you!

CHAPTER SEVEN

Lady Tina Manning/Texas

*H*ere we are in yet another chapter. We are being acquainted with 'Women of God' from nearly everywhere. These "Ladies" are alike and yet different in their style! Not one of them has the same personality, sound of voice, or look, and that is just fine. Each is a part of the beautiful flower bouquet that God made, and ON PURPOSE, God has made them UNIQUE!

I am so blessed to next *introduce to some and present to others* my own beautiful Pastor's Wife. She is married to my Superintendent (a Pastor of Pastors) and Pastor Don Manning, Sr. of the *Salvation Lighthouse Church* in Mexia, Tx.

I was blessed that she would take time out to talk with me and share her Salvation Story. Thank you for your attention. Introducing Lady Tina Manning.

"I was raised by my grandmother in Houston. I am the eldest of my siblings, and I have a sister and a brother. I was raised in the Baptist Church and in my home to go ANYWHERE else we first had to attend Church. To participate in any other activity, we had to first go to Church! As it happened, at one point, I was living in Buffalo, TX, and would visit my brother-in-law's Church service (AME) in Centreville. At that time, I was visiting around. There were other Sundays I would go to *Tucker Church of God in Christ*, in Tucker, TX. It was there that I was filled with the precious Holy Spirit back in the 80s."

I asked Lady Tina if she had ever imagined herself one day being a Pastor's Wife. She was quite clear that she NEVER wanted to ever see herself as the woman married to the Pastor. Our conversation went on.

> *I never, never wanted to be a Pastor's Wife, and I never wanted to marry a Pastor!*

"I never, never wanted to be a Pastor's Wife, and I never wanted to marry a Pastor! I was living in Houston yet attending Church. There was a young man, my Pastor's son, who was liking me, but I didn't want anything to do with him JUST BECAUSE he was the Pastor's son. Also, at the time, I was not living a Christian

lifestyle, and I did not feel ready to give up the sin that was between God and me. My auntie was a Pastor's Wife, and I had seen what she had gone through and so I didn't want to be in that position. I have not been the person to have to be up front. That's not like me. I like to sit back and enjoy; I am prayerful, and God shows me things."

> *I love the joy of being able to serve God!*

It is true that Lady Tina sits quietly, most times. She does have a "Meek 'n Quiet Spirit." She is polite and presents a warm, kind smile. Another thing about Lady Tina is her Spirit of Praise. The Praise of God seems to explode within her, and it is a blessing. I know it blesses me!

"I love the joy of being able to serve God!" Lady Tina says. When I started dating my husband, I did not know he was a Pastor's son. He nor I was living saved at that time. I was attending college in Tyler, and we met as I was moving into an apartment there. He had a friend that lived nearby, and this is how we first became acquaintances.

"A year or so later (1985), we got married. Both my husband and I had been running from the Lord. The Lord began tugging at my heart, and again, I began to attend my brother-in-law's Church. I began to see the Lord changing me."

As we continue in First Lady Tina's testimony, a tragedy happens! There was a house fire that involved extended family members, as well. Caught in the fire were children. They were cousins. Lady Tina's husband later was hospitalized with second-and third-degree burns as he was making every attempt possible to pull the children out of the window and to safety. Not all the children survived; two went on to Heaven. Needless to say, this had to have been a very hard storm to get through. Their three-year-old daughter was one of those who passed away, and their four-year-old nephew, also. Even now, we send prayers to all family members involved for God's healing and comfort to them.

"That was hard. The Lord helped me through it. I would pray, 'Lord, I gotta do better, I can't stay where I am.' God had before been tugging at my heart. Since this happened, I am doing a lot better."

As we read this, let us continue to keep this and other families in prayer who have gone through stormy situations such as this. It might have been years ago now, but we can yet pray for any lingering emotional aftermath of the crisis.

"As time has gone on, my husband and I have been serving the Lord. We were attending the Church my father-in-law Pastored. My husband's father was also a Pastor overseeing other Churches. There came a need for a Pastor in one Church, a few miles away. My father-in-law asked my husband, his eldest son, to serve there as Pastor. I really didn't want to leave *Salvation Lighthouse,* but we were obedient to our superintendent and father.

"This assignment was a challenge to us because we were younger, serving a congregation of those our senior - age-wise. Many were set in their ways, and there were issues that had to be addressed. We had the challenge of stepping into Pastoring a congregation that was yearning for their former Pastor. I remember receiving correspondence from the former Pastor's Wife (who had moved to another location with her husband); she wrote a letter to encourage me, and then there were the times our Church family from *Salvation Lighthouse* would come and visit us. I would be so glad to see them. Also, I had the example of my mother-in-law. She was an example for me in the home and for everything!"

[NICHELLE'S NOTE – 5] *Lady Tina's mother-in-law (Mother Mary Manning) is recognized and honored in the dedication page section at the front of this book. Refer to the Table of Contents for the specific chapter and page.*

"My father-in-law passed away in 2016, and it was then that we stepped officially into the position of Pastor and first Lady at *Salvation Lighthouse.*"

Yes, ma'am, I came to *Salvation Lighthouse* long after 2016; so, I never had the pleasure of meeting your father-in-law. I have heard commendable things about him, but I am thankful for the blessed job you and Pastor Manning (your husband) are doing. Thank you for the 'watch care' of my soul!

Here are a few of Lady Tina's FAVORITE THINGS:

FAVORITE PAST TIMES: Watching movies, reading, walking, window shopping, the gym occasionally.

FAVORITE SCRIPTURE: Psalm 27

FAVORITE FLOWER: Purple Tulip

VOCATION: An Educator working with elementary-aged children

FAVORITE SONG (S): *Hold On* (LeAndria Johnson) and *The battle is the Lord's* (Yolanda Adams)

WORKING IN THE CHURCH: Praise 'n worship, ushering, member of the District Choir, hospitality assistant, and Church Secretary.

Lady Tina, thank you again for sharing with us your journey this far. May God continue to bless and keep you and yours!

Salvation Lighthouse Church

915 N. Lena Street

Mexia, TX 76667

slhcogic@gmail.com

CHAPTER EIGHT

Lady Deborah Carter/Fairbanks, Alaska

ℬ eing a Pastor's Wife is not easy, but it can be rewarding. You just have to remember that you are the helpmate and not the priest of the household. We are here to support and encourage our husband.

Don't let the title determine who you are. While you are in this position, seek God for wisdom and understanding. Stay prayed up at all times. Make sure you take time out for yourself.

Without the title First Lady, we have to know that we are still somebody," says **Lady Deborah Carter** of Fairbanks, Alaska. She leaves an inspirational word to other Pastors' wives, **"Don't let the title determine who you are. While you are in this position, seek God for wisdom and understanding.** *Stay prayed up at all times. Make sure you take time out for yourself."*

We are thankful for the loving attitude Lady Deborah had in kindly giving the words above to other fellow Women of God who are serving in the role of a Pastor's Wife. Certainly, this entire book project is meant to be a source of encouragement and enlightenment to others. A spotlight is being shown on these great servants of the Most High God. They've been anointed to stand beside their anointed husband, and they are not in this specific Spiritual place by chance; they are more than a pretty face. The interview with Lady Deborah Carter continues. May I introduce you further? Meet this Pastor's Wife.

Lady Deborah, how did you come to have a relationship with Jesus and be baptized of the Holy Spirit?

There was a biblical dramatical event held one year. It was so eye-opening as it was about one's eternal destiny. That play got my attention, and I repented of my sins. Jesus saved me!

Wow, to all of those involved in drama ministries out there, it is good to know that anointed plays and skits are viable tools for winning the lost to Christ; and now, years later, you literally serve next to your husband, the Pastor.

83

By the way, how did you meet your husband, your Pastor?

"We met in Guam. At that time, we were both in the military and stationed there. For both he and I, this was our first duty station."

Oh, so you both were serving our country. Thank you both for your service in the military. And so, was he a chaplain or Pastor at that time?

"No Ma'am, he was not going to Church at all at that time," says Lady Deborah.

So, first Lady Carter, did you ever envision that you would one day be a First Lady, and was it what you thought (the role) would be? Why or why not?

I never envisioned being a Pastor's Wife at all, and I can't really say if it's what I thought it would be. Honestly, I am still learning. I do know that every First Lady's role can be slightly different in each Church congregation. So, to answer your question: "No, I really didn't know what to expect."

How long have you served in the role of a first Lady?

"We have been serving under ten years now, and I am a newbie as it relates to being a Pastor's Wife."

Yes, ma'am, so it has not been a very long time, and can you share with us, first, any challenges you have encountered? *Because maybe there is another out there new to the role of the Pastor's Wife that you can relate to.*

"Well, I must say that there have been challenges. First of all, because where I am serving, the former Pastor's Wife is yet in our congregation. There is the pressure of being who God has called me to be, especially as it relates to my husband, the Pastor, and being in the shadow of the Pastor's Wife who previously served this congregation.

"The next challenge, I would note, is when people want to dictate their opinion of what I should do, how I should act, and how they feel I should dress.

> *I truly thank God for allowing me to be me! God is continually giving me the wisdom and understanding to seek Him first.*

I truly thank God for allowing me to be me! God is continually giving me the wisdom and understanding to seek Him first. No two people are alike. I will not ever be able to satisfy everybody and their opinion. These have been challenges, BUT GOD has and is working it all out."

Is there anything you wish you had known before you became the First Lady?

"Yes, just how much people would be watching everything that I do and say.

The interview continues. Lady Carter, tell us of the joys you have experienced while in your role as the woman of God standing beside the Pastor:

"I have experienced joy in watching my husband (the Pastor), doing what I had previously heard him say was his Spiritual calling, in the *Five-fold Ministry*. I am Godly proud to see it come to pass! It brings me joy to be able to stand next to him and support him in the ministry we serve in.

> *I have experienced joy in watching my husband, (the Pastor), doing what I had previously heard him say was his Spiritual calling, in the Five-fold Ministry. I am Godly proud to see it come to pass! It brings me joy to be able to stand next to him and support him in the ministry we serve in.*

I wanted to hear more about Lady Deborah, the other roles she has served, and other hobbies or activities she may enjoy outside of the four walls of the sanctuary. Here's what she had to say:

"Well, you know, by God's grace, I have served several years as a part of the Body of Christ. I have sung in the choir, filled in as secretary when needed, attended our pulpit guests with a cool drink, and so much more. I am a servant at heart, and you might say I have the "Gift of Helps.

"For over a decade, I served in the military and then worked a civilian service career for two decades plus; until I retired officially.

"My extracurricular activities include traveling, baking, doing puzzles, walking, and crocheting."

Here are a few of Lady Deborah's FAVORITE THINGS:

FAVORITE SCRIPTURE:

"I can do all things through Christ which strengthens me" (Philippians 4:13 KJV).

"…Because I know that no matter what I am going through or what situation I may be in, that with God on my side, I can accomplish anything."

FAVORITE FLOWERS:

Red – Carnation, Yellow-Daffodil, White-Daisy

FAVORITE COLOR:

Red

I just have one more question. At the end of your earthly life, how will you want people to remember you?

"I would want them to know and recognize that I was a God-fearing woman that loved the Lord, loved people, and would do anything she could to help anyone! I would want to be remembered as faithful and willing to serve regardless of my said position."

Lady Deborah, we'd like to thank you for allowing us to highlight your walk with the Lord and for the inspired encouragement you have shared with us this day. May you be encouraged to walk on with Jesus, and may you remember that you are one of the "greatest" because of your heart for service to our Lord and his people!

DID YOU KNOW?

Olympic winning "Gold Medalist" **Sydney McGlaughlin**, of New Brunswick, NJ just said in one of her Tokyo Olympic sports interviews, by 'Access,' that if she could be or do anything other than do her sport of track, that it would be *to be a PASTOR'S WIFE.*

REPORTER: If you were not an Olympian, a professional runner, what else might you be?

Sydney McGlaughlin: My boyfriend wants to be a Pastor, so I'll probably be a Pastor's Wife when I'm done.

REPORTER: A Pastor's Wife?

Sydney McGlaughlin: Yeah!

This interview was conducted around or about August 5th (2021), and the gold medal sprinter and hurdler said it more than one time. I was blessed to see and hear this interview when I just happened to be writing our book, *MEET THE PASTOR'S WIFE.* It is such an honorable position, (The Pastor's Wife), and to hear this woman basically declare her desire to stand beside her boyfriend one day as his Wife, his helpmeet, as a Pastor's Wife; (Lord willing), this was so very nice and refreshing to hear.

In another sports interview, Ms. McGlaughlin goes on to say: "What I have in Christ is far greater than gold." God should get all the glory, for certainly no matter what, no matter where, He

89

should get all the glory for any and every accomplishment! These interviews really blessed my heart, and I thought I would spotlight them!

It is my prayer request to God that this "LADY OLYMPIAN" will one day obtain a copy of *MEET THE PASTOR'S WIFE* and be able to read every one of your chapters on standing in those shoes. (Lady Yolanda Ferguson calls them the high heels of the First Lady, Chapter four). As a matter of fact, this author would have loved to have had the privilege of interviewing (Ms. Sydney/Mrs. Sydney) on this subject. It would've been nice to get her own personal thoughts regarding her desire to be a FIRST LADY, i.e., Pastor's Wife!

Now, I must not assume that all of you keep up with Olympic happenings, so let me share with you just a little about the young Lady I just mentioned: She is a 22-year-old professional runner who is from Brunswick, NJ. She won a gold medal in the 400-meter hurdles and even broke her own record by nearly half a second, and it was a world record. (51.46). She first made the Rio Olympics at the age of 16.

May she continue to love the Lord with all her heart, mind, soul and strength, (Refer to Mark 12:30 KJV). And may God give **OLYMPIAN SYDNEY MCGLAUGHLIN** the desires of her heart!

[**UPDATE**] *This Olympian just said "Yes." She is now engaged to her fiancé, who has the goal of becoming a Pastor, as it was reported in the news. May God bless and keep them both in righteousness! May they lead MANY souls to Christ!*

CHAPTER NINE

Lady Robin Little/Tennessee

*M*y sisters and my brothers, **I WOULD LIKE TO NOW INTRODUCE TO SOME AND PRESENT TO OTHERS** a radiant 'woman of God' who I have known for many years now. In my opinion, this woman runs over with the love of the Lord, and when you see her, she approaches you with the biggest, brightest smile you have ever seen. It is not an exaggeration. When you have met and interacted with her, you will certainly see this; and when she sees you, she will see a 'Diamond! She serves as a Pastor beside her own husband, who is Senior Pastor at Diamond Ministries of Clarksville, Tennessee.

Lady Robin Little, we are going to delve into your 'salvation story.' Thank you for sharing it with us. Let's start with the joys you have had in standing with and serving beside your husband in ministry. Please share your joys with us.

I absolutely love people, and it's beautiful to unearth the jewels, (a referral to digging up diamonds before they have been polished up), so it is just a real joy just to love and shower each individual with love and kindness and to see the transformation in each person growing to know and love Jesus Christ and growing in ministry. Also, one of my greatest joys has been to witness the growth of my husband into an awesome, loving, caring Pastor and teacher of the word of God, full of confidence!

"I absolutely love people, and it's beautiful to unearth the jewels, (a referral to digging up diamonds before they have been polished up), so it is just a real joy just to love and shower each individual with love and kindness and to see the transformation in each person growing to know and love Jesus Christ and growing in ministry. Also, one of my greatest joys has been to witness the growth of my husband into an awesome, loving, caring Pastor and teacher of the word of God, full of confidence!"

Yes, ma'am, that is beautiful! Well, I met you years ago when our families were fellowshipping in the same Church congregation. Later, you were appointed as the president of the 'hospitality committee' please tell us in what other ways have you served within the body of Christ?

"Sunday School Teacher, usher, praise and worship leader, administrator, nursery aide, hospitality leader, cook, evangelist, prayer team, bus driver, outreach coordinator, leader of the Women's Department, Bible study leader, programs/fund raiser leader, and serving in the mission's department.

"We see you have served in various ways; God will not forget your labor of love; God bless you for your service to our Lord!

Let's take it back, Lady Robin. We would like to hear how your story unfolded. How did you come to know Jesus in the forgiveness of your sins and receive the precious gift of the holy Spirit?

"I came to Jesus after giving birth to my oldest son while still in high school and recognizing that for me to give him a better life, I would first have to be better, so I went to Church and got saved, delivered, and filled with the Holy Spirit; this was the Summer of 1982. I fell in love with Jesus Christ. It's been thirty-nine years of a continuing love relationship! I had met my husband previously in 1980 when neither of us was thinking of the Lord, only each other, lol."

Yes, ma'am, and we see that God had plans for you both! Did you ever envision that you'd one day be standing alongside a Pastor? And if you did, was it everything you thought it would be?

"After salvation, the Lord revealed to me that we would be Pastoring. It took almost 30 years to manifest, and it was a journey full of hard life and people lessons, and it is yet being completed. It is truly a big responsibility learning and managing the business aspect

> *I did not think that it would be so difficult dealing with people; one day they love you, and the next day they don't. I can say I am learning wisdom in conversation, studying to be quiet more, and getting to know those who labor with me in ministry.*

of the ministry. Also, I did not think that it would be so difficult dealing with people; one day, they love you, and the next day they don't. I can say I am learning wisdom in conversation, studying to be quiet more, and getting to know those who labor with me in ministry. Overall, I love Pastoring. I know God has called me to help develop His people that are willing to be developed into great disciples of Jesus Christ and, most of all, to sow seeds of love. I know God will do the rest because He is the gardener."

How long have you been married, and how long have you been serving in this particular role?

"My husband and I were at year thirty-two at the point that we began Pastoring together. I have been serving as a First Lady for about seven years now and as a Pastor for about 11 years. I have been a Wife and mother for almost 40 years now. We inherited this ministry; my husband and I were already serving as Assistant Pastors, and when our then senior Pastor had to leave, we then stepped into that role.

"Wife and mother are my greatest callings: I am Teacher, Prophetess, Evangelist, and Pastor Servant of the Highest."

Pastor Robin, you have told us about your *"joys" of unearthing diamonds*. Please tell us some of the challenges you have faced along the way.

"It has been challenging to allow people to make mistakes and learn from them within their responsibilities in ministry. It has been a challenge to love unconditionally without having an attitude -- to 'Let go and let God,' to 'Study to be quiet,' and to know that mental illness is real and to not be ashamed of asking for help! It has been a challenge to understand and recognize the enemy and to not be intimidated by the enemy knowing and being fully persuaded that God has got me and rather good or bad, everyone I encounter has a purpose!"

Amen. Amen. So, what have you learned that you wish you had known before you stepped into this ministry role?

"I learned that it is a very lonely position to be in, and there are not a lot of people I can talk to about ministry or what I am going through or have been through. I cannot always speak what I feel or know openly, and I am learning wisdom and respect even more."

Yes, Ma'am, the words you speak echos so many "ladies" in this position; I appreciate your transparency. At this time, will you say something to the first Lady in the role now and those who later may be?

"Relax and enjoy the journey and trust the conductor. 'This too shall pass.' Encourage yourself! Don't be condemned or too hard on yourself or others. Always love and forgive and stay free! You do You, be who God made you! You are not defined by a position but by your character. We are all children of God and servant leaders and give all of your cares to the Lord!"

Lady Robin, at the end of your life, how would you like to be remembered?

"I want to be remembered as a person of love for God and his people and as a servant of God full of good works."

A few of your FAVORITE THINGS:

FAVORITE COLOR(S):

White, royal blue, burgundy, and black

FAVORITE SONG(S): *Awesome God* (Brian C. Wilson), *Jesus is the Light* (Florida Mass Choir),

Everything you Touch is a Song, (Winans)

EXTRACURRICULAR ACTIVITIES:

"I am involved as a grandparent and a mom, Community Resource Advisor, Licensed Adult Educator, Licensed Cosmetologist, Professional clown, culinary arts/food service. I work with various community food service programs to give out food and other items to those in need in my community. I am learning arts and crafts, vinyl cutting, and t-shirt making, and other things good that my hands can find to do."

If your congregation were to send you and your spouse on an all-expense-paid vacation of your choice, where would it be?

I would want to return to a place we have visited before: Grand Oasis all-inclusive resort in Cancun, Mexico. We loved it!

Thank you, 'dear heart,' for sharing wisdom from your journey; despite any challenges you have or will come to face, you certainly are a blessed inspiration to all you meet. Diamond, we do see you shining! God bless you and yours!

CHAPTER TEN

Mother Sadie Mcmillan Jones/Michigan

*M*other McMillan Jones, one we would call a "Mother in Zion." With a bright, beautiful smile, a song in her heart, and a joyfulness, for how and where God has brought her! Upon having a conversation with her, one can tell that she is still very much in love with her husband, and Pastor who are one and the same. I could hear the excitement of her memory of over 65 years ago as she explained.

"He was a preacher when I met him. Already a minister. I had before seen him while working in the cotton field, but there was the time, he and another preacher were running a revival. So, we first

> *He was a preacher when I met him. Already a minister. I had before seen him while working in the cotton field, but there was the time, he and another preacher were running a revival...*

met each other while in the Church. We have now been married for 65 years and counting." Mother Jones told me.

Mother Jones, please tell us how it is that you came to accept Jesus as your personal Lord and Savior and receive the precious gift of the holy Spirit?

"You know, I was just telling that testimony, "She giggles to herself. "I was seven years old, and you know back then we children would have our own (play) Church services. We had set up service in front of my mom's house, and my cousin usually was the preacher. So, we were doing like we saw it done in Church. I

> *I felt the Spirit of the Lord overcome me; there were tears and high praise to the Lord! I started out as just a child playing, but I ended up being saved and filled with the Holy Spirit!*

was praising God and putting my heart into it, but this time it was different. I felt the Spirit of the Lord overcome me; there were tears and high praise to the Lord! I started out as just a child playing, but I ended up being saved and filled with the Holy Spirit! There was an adult preacher who saw this; he saw how I was being blessed and that the experience I was having was not fake."

100

Mother Jones continues…

"You know, before this, I had just had a personal childlike conversation with the Lord. I had told the Lord that I wanted to be saved, and then just like that, God did just that. I realized that the experience I had was more than our normal play time, Church service, and what I had experienced was different, what a blessed visitation from the Lord.

"Because I accepted the Lord at an early age, there is so much of the world that I don't know about. I know, by God's grace, that I avoided so much of the world's influence because I had given my life to Christ while a girl."

So, you and your husband married young, and you knew upfront that you were marrying a preacher?

"Yes, we married very young and have raised seven children. We are now grandparents and even great grandparents! He was preaching when I first met him, so I knew who I was marrying."

As the Pastor's Wife, Mother Jones, could you tell us some of the ways you supported your husband – the Pastor?

"Over the years, I have been a musician, playing piano and singing for the congregation, as well. As the children came along, they began to sing too."

Have there been challenges in your position as the Pastor's Wife?

"Were there challenges? Yes, yes, there were many challenges, and honestly, there still are. My husband is yet the Pastor, and I am the Pastor's Wife, and over the years, I have learned some things.

"Well, you know, as the First Lady, you've got to learn how to sit back, see, and don't see some things that would really upset you. You have to PRAY!" Mother Jones emphasizes, "PRAY, PRAY, PRAY!"

Mother Jones goes on to be clear about the challenges she has encountered as a First Lady and wisdom for the journey in this particular role.

> *A Pastor's Wife has got to learn how to carry herself properly before the public, because she is being watched…*

"The Pastor's Wife many times suffers from the rudeness of others, I know I did many times over the years. There has been jealousy, pettiness, rudeness shown toward me as the First Lady. Sometimes the Pastor's Wife has been blamed for things that did not go as planned. A Pastor's Wife has got to learn how to carry herself properly before the public; because she is being watched, so, to the Pastor's Wives out there, be mindful of the attitude you have. It takes the Holy Spirit to make it; it takes 'Temperance.'

"You should not show your weakness before the public. If you and your husband are going through something, it is not for the entire congregation to see. I learned to discuss and find solutions for my Pastor husband and me privately, and we would not discuss those things out of the public eye; and AGAIN, a Pastor's Wife must be a woman of Prayer."

You should not show your weakness before the public. If you and your husband are going through something, it is not for the entire congregation to see. I learned to discuss and find solutions for my Pastor husband and me privately, and we would not discuss those things out of the public eye; and AGAIN, a Pastor's Wife must be a woman of Prayer.

[NICHELLE'S NOTE – 6] *There are times a Pastoral couple needs Christian counseling, and I don't believe any couple should continue to let things fester or be unsolved between them. There should be a trusted overseer, a couple you both are neutrally accountable to that maybe can intervene between you two, but I so agree with Mother Jones that personal issues should not be hung out before the congregation you Pastor. In my opinion, it could only make things worse. They are not all Spiritually equipped /Christians mature enough to deal with what they are going through and what their leaders are going through at the same time.*

Mother Jones mentioned how busy it can get for a Pastoral couple; the scheduled Church meetings and such and while raising children.

"Once the children were old enough to stay at the house by themselves, my Pastor husband and I learned how to jump into the car (after he had returned from work) and take a drive." Mother Jones begins to smile as she talks about this:" We would just enjoy the time together. That was the time I could fill him in with all that he may have needed to know about my day and to talk about whatever was not for the children's ears. We would just talk, just he and I, and enjoy our drive. This is something we have done down through the years, and I have wonderful memories of it."

103

Lady Jones, if your Church congregation were to send you and the Pastor on an all-expense paid-for vacation, where would you want to travel to?

Although she touched on going on a cruise, Mother Jones later changed her answer to Hawaii.

Favorite song:

To God Be The Glory, For The Things He Has Done

Favorite color:

Purple (representing royalty)

Favorite pastimes:

In years past, sewing, keeping the house, and keeping up with the children.

Mother Jones, please share with us more of what you'd like to say to another Pastor's Wife, please.

"Remain prayerful and keep each other reminded that you are to be a God-fearing example before the people, even when someone is disrespectful and has a bad attitude toward you. Be brave! Don't talk too much. Don't discuss other people's business, and don't discuss your own personal business with others. If we talk too much, then before we know it, others will have it all out in the streets, and the origin was you. Don't let that be said of you. First, pray about what to do about things that perplex you."

[NICHELLE'S NOTE – 7] *See a professional Christian Counselor if necessary.*

First Lady Sadie McMillan Jones comes back to say, to emphasize.

Never talk to others concerning your husband and the personal business between you two! 'My husband is off limits!' Whatever is going on between him and me is between he and me.

"Never talk to others concerning your husband and the personal business between you two! 'My husband is off limits!' Whatever is going on between him and I is between he and me."

God bless you, Mother Jones. We appreciate you sharing from your heart and experience.

Congratulations on your 65 years of marriage! God bless you and yours!

SEVEN MISTAKES A PASTOR'S WIFE SHOULD NOT MAKE

1. **Don't fight the Church.**

    "How can you fight God's Wife? The Church is God's bride, His Wife, and you are a part of that. Your husband has a call to the Church that he has to fulfill, so if you fight the Church, you will not win."

2. **Don't misunderstand the concept of hospitality.**

    "Hospitality is not the same thing as access. You cannot allow just anyone into your home. Your home is NOT the Church. Everyone should not have access to your children; everyone should not be allowed into your home. Use wisdom."

3. **Thinking that you belong to the Church.**

    "Not everyone will love you because you are the Pastor's Wife, but you must love everyone because you are the Pastor's Wife. You should not have a feeling of entitlement toward all the congregation simply because you are the Pastor's Wife. It's a privilege and honor IF they should do nice things for you."

4. **Thinking prayer is optional. You cannot do marriage, ministry, or life successfully without PRAYER!** *"Your husband is in ministry, which makes him an automatic target of the devil. Your husband is building God's kingdom, fighting for God's house, teaching people the Word, and the devil has an agenda. As a Pastor's Wife, you must pray!" Prayer is not optional!"*

107

5. **Don't forget that you live in a glass house.**

"Remember that your life is out there on display, whether you like it or not. Those who live in glass houses don't throw stones. Package yourself well. Package your husband and children well. Anything you don't want to be repeated, don't say. People are watching you. You are a standard-setter.

6. **Live for an audience of one.**

"This is your biggest assignment! People are not more important than God. Know who sent you, what He sent you to do, and do that. Your first job is to be the Pastor's Wife. Don't forget to Wife your husband. Be a help to your husband. If he changed from being a Pastor, would you still be essential in his life as a Wife?"

7. **Never make the mistake of forgetting that your husband is first a man.**

"Don't say things like, 'How could you, Pastor?' Don't put him on a pedestal. He is a man. He has needs. All men can be tempted. Your husband is first a man before he is a 'Man of God.'"

[NICHELLE'S NOTE – 8] *The teaching this beautiful "Lady" gave on this subject was so insightful. I took notes and shared them here with you! I give LADY MILDRED KINGSLEY-OKONKWO full credit for having said and taught this via her YOUTUBE channel: "Mentoring Sessions with Pastor "M." FACEBOOK: LADY MILDRED KINGSLEY-OKONKWO*

I only gave excerpts. Please watch to get the full teaching.

CHAPTER ELEVEN

Lady Lisa McDaniel/California

$\mathcal{W}$e serve many different types of people that come from many different backgrounds while Pastoring. Many are broken or have been betrayed. They have a hard time trusting. Some are afraid to love, show love, and even be loved. Love is a powerful

> *Showing them Christ's love and how much He loves them through me is my goal, no matter the situation or outcome.*

emotion. It requires faithfulness and commitment. Showing them Christ's love and how much He loves them through me is my goal, no matter the situation or outcome."

Meet **Lady Lisa McDaniel** of the state of California. She gives us a nutshell version of her experience with the people of her congregation and her personal goal to show God's love to all.

Lady Lisa, it is a pleasure to meet your acquaintance! Thank you for allowing us to hear the testimony of your Christian journey. We will start by asking, how did you come to know Jesus and receive the precious gift of the Holy Spirit?

"I gave my heart to the Lord over the phone with a Pastor's Wife, and my life changed at that very moment. As I came out of the water, during Water Baptism, I received the Holy Spirit with the gift of tongues."

Hallelujah! What a blessing!

How long, First Lady Lisa, have you been the Pastor's Wife?

"I have served ten years as a First Lady but have been in ministry for over thirty-five years."

That is amazing, thirty-five years? So, please tell us how you met your husband, your Pastor.

"When my husband and I met, neither of us were Christians. We have now been married for 42 years."

Did you ever envision that you would one day be a Pastor's Wife, and was it what you thought (the role) would be? Why or why not?

> *I wish I had known that everyone that you love will not love you back.*

"Once I became a Christian, I felt a calling. Yes and no. Yes, doing the Lord's work has been rewarding, but no, it also comes with great heartache and loneliness."

Please, share with us what you have learned as the first Lady that you wish you had known before you stepped into the role.

"I wish I had known that everyone that you love will not love you back. There isn't just one moment or situation that I can recall. I asked God to remove those things from my memory. Even though they were hard, I chose to allow them to be a part of my growth. I just know that being a First Lady is a call. When God calls the husband into a ministry of Pastorship over a Church, God prepares his Wife to be his helper as well. That role can take on many parts. Some of those parts are joyful, and

some are very painful. It is all a part of ministry. But God guides us through if we let Him. I must always rely on God's leading through the Holy Spirit and prayer."

We appreciate you, Lady Lisa, you're being honest with us and sharing your heart.

112

So, tell us, is your husband the founding Pastor, or are you two the founders of this particular Church congregation?

"We stepped into a ministry that was already established, but it was bruised and broken. So we have had to build it from the ground up.

"In the Church that we were mentored in, we served in many areas of ministry while we were there for approximately fifteen years. We served under the Pastor and Wife, who held the ministry there. It was a larger Church. We were just servants and were very hungry to learn and serve however God wanted us to. These Pastors were our mentors, and even though they are now in their young 90 s today and live on the other side of the USA, they still have a huge role in our lives. We communicate regularly over the phone.

"Once they retired, God called us to what I call ground ministry. So, we did some traveling and ministered in different Churches of all sizes and places for a while.

> *I must always rely on God's leading through the Holy Spirit and prayer."*

"Then we settled for another short while in another small Church that brought us closer to home base. But again, it was just for a short time, a time of preparation for what was coming next. There my husband was being prepared while serving as an associate for the next stage of our calling. There I was being prepared as I served in many areas of ministry, mostly I counseled young women when there was a need. Then in a short time of being there, God called us to the Church we are now as the senior Pastors where God wanted us to be.

"We love our Church, and still at times, are asked to speak occasionally at different Pastor friends of ours' Church congregations."

113

Yes, I see it's been quite an equipping journey! In your role, are you called by any other title than First Lady?

"Yes, sometimes I am called Mrs. Pastor."

I like that, so Mrs. Pastor, please give us some of the joys you have experienced in the role of a Pastor's Wife.

"Mentoring and disciplining women who have a desire to go deeper in God by His word. This brings great joy to my heart."

In what capacity (roles, auxiliaries, jobs) have you ever served in or out of your Church congregation?

"I was an assistant in children's Church ministries for many years. I made myself available to any area that there was a need."

Lady Lisa, you have the opportunity to say something to all of those who will read this book. We would like for your voice to be heard. What would you like to say to them?

> *Always keep your focus on the Lord.*

"Always keep your focus on the Lord. People will leave you and fail you because they are people, but God will never leave you nor forsake you. He would leave the 99 for just one. That's how much he loves!

114

Lady Lisa, when all is said and done, and your life on earth has ended, what would you like to be remembered for?

"I want people to remember that I was faithful until the end! And I also want them to remember that I loved my family."

A few of your FAVORITE THINGS:

EXTRACURRICULAR ACTIVITIES:

"I enjoy gardening, cooking, and spending time with my grandbabies, of which I have four."

> *I want people to remember that I was faithful until the end! And I also want them to remember that I loved my family.*

FAVORITE COLORS:

"I like turquoise and purple."

FAVORITE SONG(S):

"One of my favorite songs is *Reckless Love*. I believe that song was written about my life (Spiritually speaking). Another song I favor is *Oceans*. The part of the song that says, 'You call me out upon the waters, the great unknown,' is a verse which reminds me that's where I find Him, in the mysteries of the deep."

If a flower were to represent you, which one would it be?

"Evening primrose, yellow is a flower that represents me. It only blooms at night, so only certain people will notice it. But it's yellow and has a lemon scent."

FAVORITE SCRIPTURE: Matthew 25:40: "When you reach out to those who are the forgotten ones, or the down and out, and the lonely, Jesus says, "You've done it unto me."

Thank you, and God bless you and yours, Lady Lisa McDaniel. Be encouraged. God will not forget your "labor of love."

CHAPTER TWELVE

Lady Dianne Manning/Texas

remember when I was a young girl, my great grandmother would take us to Beulah Baptist Church in Wortham, Texas. My memories are mostly of Easter. I remember her singing, "he rose, he rose he rose from the dead…." Then after my mom married and we moved to Fairfield to live with my stepfather, I was in the fourth grade. We joined his Church, which was Fairfield Missionary Baptist Church. My mom would take us to all the local Churches in the area when they were having their summer revivals.

"I will never forget I was in the 6th grade when I had my first encounter with the Lord. We attended a revival at Hemphill Temple, Church of God in Christ (COGIC), and I knew the Lord saved me. I remember the kids in my class making fun of me when I told them that I was saved. "

Amen, God bless you! Meet **Lady Dianne Manning** of the 'Lone Star State' of Texas, also known as Evangelist Dianne Manning. Full of the Holy Spirit, full of Christ's love, and on fire for the Lord, indeed! Lady Dianne is an Anointed Sunday School Teacher! I am blessed to have sat in her Sunday School

> *I will never forget I was in the 6th grade when I had my first encounter with the Lord. We attended a revival at Hemphill Temple COGIC, and I knew the Lord saved me. I remember the kids in my class making fun of me when I told them that I was saved.*

class and have benefited Spiritually as a result of it. Her "Preacher" stands up many times as she is teaching, and it's all good!   I am honored to be a part of the same Church congregation that she is—the Salvation Lighthouse Church.

She is my assistant Pastor's Wife and known to be a dynamic evangelistic speaker in the local area where we all live. She teaches our Sunday School class most times at the Salvation Lighthouse Church and, in her anointed teaching, consistently reminds us that we are 'The Salt and the Light' of this world. So, 'I now present to some and introduce to others' Lady Dianne Manning. Please receive her. She continues to tell us of how she met "JESUS."

"Then, later after I married and started going to Church with my in-laws, my experience with the Lord began to come back. I was attending a revival at Tucker COGIC, and after I got home that night, I was saying my prayer, and the Spirit of the Lord came upon me. I began to speak with other tongues. I remember getting up because I was on my knees. I went into the bathroom because I didn't want to wake my husband, and I tried to stop speaking in other tongues, but I couldn't. It was the greatest feeling I ever had up to that point."

> *I was attending a revival at Tucker COGIC, and I after I got home that night, I was saying my prayer and the Spirit of the Lord came upon me. I began to speak with other tongues…*

What a beautiful experience that had to be! So now it is that you are an evangelist and the assistant Pastor's Wife at your home Church congregation. Tell us how you met your husband?

"From the 9th grade all thru high school, my husband and my lockers were side-by-side. We would see each other at some point every day. So, our junior year is when we became boyfriend and girlfriend. We got married on January 30, 1981, and have been together for over 40 years. He is the love of my life!"

I so much enjoy hearing these two do what I call a 'Tag-team ministry type of thing,' not that it is planned nor set up that way officially. It's just that she teaches the Sunday School under God's anointing, and in our Sunday School Review of Lesson, her husband (our assistant Pastor takes to the podium (as if they are tag-teaming the enemy) and puts the 'Icing on the Cake,' so to speak! We are blessed so through this dedicated couple!

Lady Dianne, was your husband (Pastor Richie) Pastoring or ministering before you met him, and had you ever envisioned yourself being a Pastor's Wife?

"No. He was the assistant Pastor for the following Churches: Rocky Mount Baptist Church and a (Church) in Oakwood, Texas. He Pastored White Temple's Church in Elkhart, Texas. He is currently serving as Assistant Pastor of Salvation Lighthouse COGIC in Mexia, TX.

"I don't think I envisioned being a First Lady, but I have always envisioned my husband and me working in the ministry together. I got saved before my husband, and I always prayed that the Lord would save him too! I always quoted that scripture in I Corinthian 7:14, "for the unbelieving husband is sanctified in the Wife." And I am living the answer to that prayer! It has been five years now since I have been in this specific role.

"My role has been more of a Pastor and co-Pastor. My greatest joy is working together, teaching, training, and building people in the Word. My husband has always supported me. Even though it is more acceptable in most ministries now for a woman to be Pastors and preachers, I can say he encouraged me to do what God called me to do even when it was not acceptable. And it really inspired me in ways that I could never put into words. It is one of our greatest desires to see the people of God mature in the body of Christ."

Yes, Ma'am, it was brought to my attention that you have served as a Pastor at two Churches previously. Thank you for your service to the Lord, both then and now and in the days to come!

On that note, would you please share with us some of the challenges you may have encountered?

"Staying encouraged. It's hard to see how people disrespect the man of God, and then there are the feelings of being under-appreciated."

Lady Dianne, you do work outside of the home? Please tell us what it is you do or have done in the past?

"I have held the following positions in the secular job market: I was the office manager at KNES Radio Station for ten years, I worked for Freestone County for 20 years holding the following jobs: Justice of Peace Clerk, County and District Court Coordinator, and Chief Deputy County Clerk. I currently work as a Job Requisition Coordinator for Mexia, State Supported Living Center (SSLC). I assist in the finance department, teach Sunday School, and manage the Building Fund account at my local Church."

Amazing! It is simply amazing how God has graced you to do and balance so much over the journey of your life. God indeed has you out in our local community as 'Salt 'n Light.' Thank you for representing God in such a God-fearing way!

We must also mention that Lady Dianne was also the co-owner in the 'Especially for You' resale shop. She enjoys exercising, reading, and cooking.

Amen! We are getting to know those who 'Labor among us.' What a blessed opportunity this has been. We also asked Lady Dianne to leave some encouraging words to her sisters in the faith. This is what she had to say.

"Be faithful in your relationship to the Lord. You cannot always measure it by how you feel. Go to a Church that is teaching and preaching the pure Word of God."

Be faithful in your relationship to the Lord. You cannot always measure it by how you feel. Go to a Church that is teaching and preaching the pure Word of God.

A Few of Lady Dianne's FAVORITE THINGS:

FAVORITE COLORS:

Black and turquoise

FAVORITE SONGS:

Take Me to the King and *This Joy That I Have*

If the Church congregation were ever to send you and your husband on an all-expense-paid vacation, where would you want to go?

Italy

FAVORITE FLOWERS:

Daisies, tulips

FAVORITE SCRIPTURE:

Psalm 34:1 "I will bless the Lord at all times, his praise shall continually be in my mouth..." "It's my favorite scripture because when I am praising God no matter what is going on in my life, it makes me feel better."

Psalm 34:1 just happens to be this author's favorite Bible Scripture, as well. I love it! THANK YOU, Lady Dianne Manning, for standing and speaking for "Jesus." Many are blessed by it!

CHAPTER THIRTEEN

Lady Susan Young/California

*O*ur Father's House Church is a vibrant and growing congregation that is 'Growing in grace and the knowledge of our Lord Jesus Christ,' there in the San Joaquin Valley town of Los Banos, California. Right over the hill from San Jose and a couple of hours, give or take, from the San Francisco Bay area. Los Banos is a place dear to this author, for it is my hometown! It is a farming town that has grown up a bit since I was raised there, though I would say it still has a small-town footprint. I lived there from the age of four until at least 19 years of age. My family is yet there as well as many other friends and family.

The 'Woman of God' we will interview here in Chapter Twelve is a Spiritual mover and shaker therein "Our Father's House." The services on Sunday are "Live" streamed, and I am sure you would be blessed watching if you were not in your own services. She stands beside her husband, the senior Pastor there, and they both wear the title Pastor. I am especially blessed by this "Lady" because my daughter is a parishioner there at the Church. My eldest daughter has been a part of the ministry there for several years now, and I know that this beautiful soul has positively influenced my daughter and others.

And so, it is my pleasure to 'Introduce To Most, And Present To Others,' Lady Susan Young.

Thank you again for being a part of our 'Meet 'n Greet' Lady Young. I am going to pretty much let you flow and tell us your 'Salvation Story' and *Overcoming* testimony.

> *I was raised Catholic and converted to the Protestant faith in 1992 when I attended a Charismatic Pentecostal Church...*

Let's start by asking how you came to know Jesus as your personal Lord and Savior?

"I was raised Catholic and converted to the Protestant faith in 1992 when I attended a Charismatic Pentecostal Church. My husband and I attended Church in Los Banos, and our Pastor and his Wife assigned us to family ministry small groups.

> *The Pastor's Wife passed away, and we watched him fall apart. Being members of the Church, we helped where necessary to keep things together as he grieved. I remember telling my husband that our Pastor's pain was hard to watch, and I said, "I hope I die before you because I never want to be him." A few months later, my husband died, and I was left in the same state as our Pastor.*

"The Pastor's Wife passed away, and we watched him fall apart. Being members of the Church, we helped where necessary to keep things together as he grieved. I remember telling my husband that our Pastor's pain was hard to watch, and I said, "I hope I die before you because I never want to be him." A few months later, my husband died, and I was left in the same state as our Pastor. After some time, my Pastor asked me out for a date, and the rest was history. Before this, he had been ministering for at least ten years before we'd met."

Lady Susan continues.

"I never thought I would be a First Lady. It was never on my radar to date a Pastor. I remember when we were dating, I said, 'I don't want my role in the Church to change. I am marrying Doug Young; I am not marrying the Pastor.' His reply was, 'It's not that simple. My calling is ministry, and I gave my life to the Lord a long time ago. You can't separate me out like that.' I still thought I would figure out a way.

"At a retreat shortly after our marriage, I kneeled in the chapel, and I asked the Lord for direction. A woman I had never seen before came up to me and gave me a word from the Lord, and I still remember it today. She said, "The Lord says, 'I call whom I call. I have called you, and your

127

husband's ministry will move forward when you step into your place beside him in the Church." She didn't know me, didn't know my struggles but God was clear."

This is a unique introduction to this role. Let's hear more.

"I had a unique introduction as First Lady. I had been a member of the Church before I was First Lady, so it was in some ways easier and other ways harder.

Yes, Ma'am, how long have you served in the role of a Pastor's Wife?

"Nineteen years."

Beautiful! That is a long time of faithfulness to the Lord. I am sure in that amount of time, you have had some challenges. Would you mind sharing some of them with us?

"I wasn't raised in a ministry family, and there were no mentors in the beginning of my marriage. I didn't know that I would be like a politician's Wife. We must be careful with our opinion. We must know our place. We will be criticized for what we do, what we wear, how we raise our children. The expectations of our roles will be as vast and varied as the congregation. And the truth is some will purposefully be kind to you or purposefully mean to you to get the attention of the Pastor. We walk a tightrope in many ways."

Lady Susan, using a 'tightrope' is such a great way of explaining the walk of a First Lady among the Church's congregation. 'Walking a Tightrope' is a phrase that says so much, and I am sure many Pastors' wives would agree with you.

128

Please, also give us some of the joys of the role you stand in, besides your husband, the senior Pastor.

"Watching lives transformed is my greatest joy. I absolutely love women's ministry. Watching a woman come in with the shame and pressure that the world puts on her and then watching her transformation and realization that she is a beautiful daughter of God.

"Watching my husband's sphere of influence as he has been a Pastor in our city for almost 30 years and the difference he has made in our community by his obedience to the Lord, I realize I married the Senior Pastor, but my husband has served as an Outreach Pastor, Pastor of Evangelism, Assistant Pastor, Senior Pastor, and now Bishop.

In what capacity (roles, auxiliaries, jobs, and such) have you ever served in within or without your Church congregation?

"I was ordained in 2006 and am the Executive Pastor, and that is just a fancy name for handling the staff and administration of our Church. As any First Lady, I am sure, I have served in children's ministry, youth, marriage ministries, and wherever needed.

"I am a director of our local chapter of an organization called 'Helping One Woman.' I volunteered up until 2020 at our local high schools teaching leadership classes for girls."

Now that blesses me. It is definitely a myth when some think these women merely sit in a chair and look pretty. They are so much more. They do (for the Lord) so much more, and God is getting the glory out of their lives! I would have loved for my daughters to have been in one of her classes on leadership while at school. We need more 'Women of God' of all roles to make an impact in our general community.

And, I must say about the phrase and title, 'Helping one woman,' we can all help one –
somebody. We may not help dozens, hundreds, or thousands at a time, but maybe if we would start
with helping one person at a time, again, that blessed my thoughts.

**Pastor Young, what have you learned as the First Lady that you wish you had known before you
stepped into the role?**

> *... the point of a life in ministry is not
> to make everyone happy. My main
> responsibility is to minister to the
> man of God. Everything takes its
> place after that calling.*

"That the point of a life in ministry is not to make
everyone happy. My main responsibility is to minister to
the man of God. Everything takes its place after that
calling.

**Yes, Ma'am, and would you please say something to all of those who will read this book? What
would you want them to hear from you, expressly?**

"First Lady, you were chosen and called by the Lord, and you possess all that is needed to fulfill
your role. The enemy will come at you to try to take you off course. He knows that if he can get you off
your game, your husband loses focus, and the Church suffers. Pray diligently.

The role of the First Lady can be one of loneliness but know this for sure, The Lord himself will
minister to your tender heart. He will be your Great Defender."

Pastor Susan, at the end of your life on Earth, how would you want people to remember you?

"I would want to be remembered as someone who did her best to represent the "Father. Mostly,
I hope my family speaks well of me."

Lady Susan, if your Church congregation wanted to send you and your hubby on an all-expense vacation, where would you choose to go?

"We love the beach, and we love the mountains, so either would be fantastic!"

Before we close out this chapter, we would like to list just a few of Lady Susan's Favorite Things:

FAVORITE COLOR:

Red

FAVORITE SONG(S):

It is Well with My Soul, and *I Don't Want to Go* by Avalon

FAVORITE FLOWER(S):

Bird of Paradise. It is colorful, striking and the name itself speaks to me.

FAVORITE SCRIPTURE:

"For I am persuaded that neither death nor life, nor angels nor rulers, nor things present nor things to come, nor powers, nor height nor depth, nor any other created thing will be able to separate us from the love of God that is in Christ Jesus our Lord" Romans 8:38-39 (CSB).

"It is my reminder that no matter what, the Lord will never let go of me."

Thank you very much for your service to Christ, Lady Susan, and for sharing with us. On a personal note, I thank you and your husband for watching over the soul of my daughter there at "Our Father's House." God bless you!

131

Our Father's House

1005 "I" Street, Los Banos, CA 93635

CHAPTER FOURTEEN

Lady Patricia Prunty/California

n San Francisco, at a rap concert, I was led to the Lord by a 'Woman of God' now deceased. She was a true prophetess and introduced me to the Lord. When she prayed for me, I had this experience that changed my life immediately. I felt the gifts of God begin to pour into me! It started me on a quest of searching for more of God and a better understanding of these things.

Spiritual gifts that I had not realized before began to operate in my life. In passing people, I would know their personal business. Even as much as their name, even when I did not know them personally. I would hear, 'Tell them this.' And what I would tell them would be on point. They would be amazed, and so would I. "

I now introduce to some and present to others Lady Patricia Prunty. Her story is quite a roller coaster, but God is everywhere in it! Please listen in as she continues to give her testimony:

"The first time I met my husband, I was in the hospital. You see, over a period, I had miscarried four times. My now husband was the Pastor who had done a hospital visitation and had prayed for me. They kept putting me in hospital rooms with women who had children, and I was hurting, struggling with depression. At the time this happened, he was married to someone else, and I was too married to another. As God would have it, we would cross paths at another time in different situations.

"I was married to an adulterous man who did not understand the changes happening in me. Being young in the Lord, I was trying to make him be what I thought he should be, and it did not work.

He could not grasp what was happening to me. So many people were now following me, my parents were angry with me. I just was trusting the Bible! I trusted the Words I was reading. In time, my first husband was no longer in the home, and my marriage with him was over."

So, Lady Prunty, how did you again meet who is now your husband and Pastor?

> *It was one day as I sat in the pew that Pastor Prunty (now Bishop Prunty) walked up to me and said, 'You're gonna be my Wife ...*

"At Church. We met at Church. He had started a Church in Stockton, CA. Even before, when in my first marriage, God had told me that I would marry a Pastor, but I had misunderstood thinking my first husband was to be that one. It was one day as I sat in the pew that Pastor Prunty (now Bishop Prunty) walked up to me and said, 'You're gonna be my Wife." I responded with, 'I don't think so.' He was serious, though. He was and is a person with a beautiful and well-mannered Spirit. He is very quiet-natured in his way. He was and is a person that conversates back and forth with God, literally hearing God. He depends on God! It was almost a year from then that he proposed to me, and we are yet together.

Yes, ma'am, and now you all have been married forty-five years. That's amazing!

"Over the years, I have raised at least thirteen children. His, and mine, all together, and several children that were given over to me from relatives and otherwise. My baby brother was given to me to raise, and we raised him as my son. Another close relative of mine had four children. Three were born addicted to drugs, and the court system gave them to us. All of these know us as mom and dad. We have a large family, and there is much love between us. I am a mother always!"

Mother Prunty, please tell us about any challenges you faced after being married to your hubby and Pastor over the years.

> *I trust my husband, but sometimes women try to take advantage of my husband's quietness...*

"Women have a hard time trusting other women. So many have an agenda. I trust my husband, but sometimes women try to take advantage of my husband's quietness. They (certain women) may not see me, but I'm there, watching and looking out for my husband! They think they can get over on him, being flirtatious with him, but there is trust. I once had to talk to a woman about her behavior as it concerned my husband. She was a single woman spreading falsehood throughout the Church, and I went to her regarding this."

Yes, ma'am, and what advice would you like to give to another Pastor or minister's Wife?

"Lift him up, support him! He's gonna have much coming at him. This is a joint thing; you might have to carry a lot of the load at home. Help (your husband, the Pastor) to balance the load of home and ministry. There was a time when he was gone all the time. I had to be supportive of that, and the times I missed him, I told him so.

> *Sometimes I had to put my foot down! Because there were times I needed him to be there for me...*

"Sometimes I had to put my foot down! Because there were times, I needed him to be there for me. You should have a date night and not let anything insignificant interfere with that. 'You have to take care of the couple.' You must make provision for just you and him! Ask him for that one day (for you and him alone). Just ask him for one day."

137

Tell us of some of the capacities you have worked in and about the body of Christ.

Sunday School for varying ages, I raised children for years; it comes easy to me. Women's group and teaching women, I do my best to meet a woman where she is; teaching her to love herself; giving her the foundation she needs. I work with single women who are trying to find themselves.

"I love to declare to them: "All right, it's a new day! Your steps have already been ordered! Take off in praise! Let's Go!"

Please, tell us more of what you tell the ladies you mentor there in your congregation.

"Just stop! Take a deep breath! (Think) What could I have done better! We're the example! Be a Word Woman, give God back His Word! Do what the written Word says. You can have joy even in death. We have at the Church 'Clean and Pray.' We go to the Church, and we pray for a while. We clean for a while. If I know a sister is having a hard time, I invite her to come down to the Church with me, and we'll clean and pray, pray, and clean."

I could tell that Mother Prunty was very much in love with her husband and Pastor. She talks very highly of him and her caring for him.

"There is a 16-year difference between my husband, and 'til this day my husband will look me and say, 'I love you girl!' He makes me blush, and there are times he will find a song that plays the sentiments of his heart for me. It might be a musical excerpt on YOUTUBE. It could be on one of the westerns he has watched. My husband has such a gentle, loving heart. We don't say HAPPY 45TH ANNIVERSARY. We say HAPPY 45TH HONEYMOON. It makes us think of our emotions flooding back up, love and youthfulness, in the moment NOW! We are still having honeymoons!"

While we are on the subject, First Lady, what do you say to your peers regarding honoring their husbands?

"Don't go to bed with anything hanging over you! Keep laughter close to you. When I think I am angry at my husband, he makes me laugh. If he makes me laugh, it's over. For my husband and me, when the day has passed, it's time for the body and mind to relax. We put our truth out there, discussing whatever we need to discuss. 'This is how I took it, and this is what I meant.' Human to human."

Thank you so much, Lady Prunty! In our interview, we discussed so much. This chapter does not capture all of your overcoming testimony, but we have tried to put some of it in a nutshell.

Here are a few of your FAVORITE THINGS:

FAVORITE COLOR:

Red

FAVORITE PASTIME:

I don't do it anymore, but I used to be a seamstress. I enjoy being around children, around the youth – we connect well. I have raised so many children. One should not spend all their time scolding, just give them a foundation, steer them with wisdom! God uses me in the gifts of Word of Knowledge, Word of Wisdom, Discernment of the Spirit. I teach and sing.

Mother Prunty, if your congregation were to send you and your hubby on an all-expense-paid vacation, where would you want to go?

I would want to go to Jonesboro, Arkansas, so my husband could go and visit his brothers.

FAVORITE SCRIPTURE:

I have been crucified with Christ; and it is no longer I that live, but Christ lives in me: and that life which I now live in the flesh I live in faith, the faith, which is in the Son of God, who loved me, and gave himself up for me" Galatians 2:20 (ASV).

Amazing, Lady Prunty. Our God is amazing! You are one who empowers. May God bless and keep you and yours!

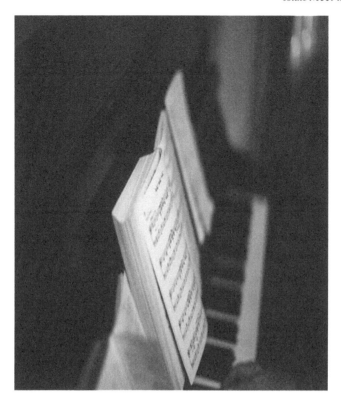

STEREOTYPES OF THE PASTOR'S WIFE

1. **They all know how to play the piano.**

    This is just NOT true.

2. **They all wear big hats.**

    All First Ladies have their own sense of style. Not all of them wear hats. Hats are beautiful and in great taste, but not all wear them, and a Pastor's Wife does not have to.

3. **Their house is your house, and the 'Church membership' should have full access.**

    This is just not true. It is very presumptuous of anyone to assume that they have access to someone else's private home. Preacher's wives, people have various motives for wanting to come into your home. Hospitality does not have to be at any moment a parishioner chooses and wants to come by suddenly. Your home is your family's private place, and you need someplace, just for you and yours! **#Guardyourhome**

4. **They all wear 'Red Bottom' shoes.** Wearing a certain brand of shoe is a preference and depends on a "Lady's" budget as well; not all Pastor's wives have the same budget. Pastor's Wife, you can look like a million bucks and not have spent millions.

142

5. **They all wear 'St. John' suits**

    Again, the wives of Pastors do not all have the same budget, and all are at different stages in the ministry. Most would not refuse the congregation presenting to them the gift of a St. John suit, so if you have an unction to Bless her sweetly, Amen.

6. **Their children belong to the Church membership, and all the members should have access to them.**

    No ma'am/no sir, the Pastor and First Lady's children are *their* children, and not everybody's. The congregation is made up of recovering 'sinners,' and not all are fully delivered from sin. The Church is a hospital, true, and a place where those coming to Jesus are welcome, but no way should everyone have access to their children or grandchildren. To do so would be putting your children in a dangerous position. ALSO, even when having guests over to the house, be mindful always to supervise your children and grandchildren.

7. **A Pastor's Wife should be over the Women's Department.**

    God uses Pastors' wives in various ways and places, and there is no *cookie-cutter, one size fits all* kind of formula for the First Lady's responsibilities. Where and how the First Lady serves is at the prayerful discretion of the Pastor and his Wife, not the congregation to decide.

8. **They should NEVER miss a Church setting.**

    First Lady, God knows your personal business. Certainly, people look to see you as part of the leadership; but you are a Church member too, and there are times you will not be there for valid reasons your Pastor and husband know of. It is not mandatory that the congregation know all your personal business.

9. **Their children should act and behave perfectly.**

I have not ever seen *anybody's* underaged child behave perfectly, entirely. Children are being molded and trained on what to do and how to do it. There are times children kick against the prick, so, to speak. The Pastor and First Lady's children are no exception. THEN, when ministry-raised children grow up, they make their own decision to sell out to God or not. Yes, the right training and teaching are in them if you give it to them, but how they submit to it may vary from PK (preacher's child) to PK. Church congregation pray for your Pastor's children just like you want them to pray for yours.

10. **They all sing solos.**

Yet another stereotype! We don't all (as humans) do anything. Certainly, we all should make a 'joyful noise' (Psalm 100), and our song is to the Lord; but not all First Ladies sing sermonic solos.

CHAPTER FIFTEEN

Lady Trina Curry/Mississippi

$\mathcal{F}$irst, as I begin **Lady Trina Curry's** chapter, I would like to take this written opportunity to thank her for her service in the Army of her beloved country! She is "A soldier in the army of the lord" and

has served in America's Army as well. Lady Trina, thank you so much, for your service, in both!

Lady Trina has long since put away her green Army fatigues, and as you meet and interact with her, you will notice that she does wear "The whole armour of God" Ephesians 6:10-18 (KJV). She now serves faithfully beside her husband, the Pastor. Lady Trina is a Pastor's Wife, and we wanted to know her back story. We wanted to hear her own overcoming testimony, so come on, read along and let's get to know the Lovely Lady Trina Curry!

Well, I asked her how it was that she came to know Jesus and of her baptism in the Holy Spirit (These are her own quoted words).

I was running from God, but you cannot run from God. He knows where you are. While I was in the military as a soldier, I attended a club, and I heard a voice saying, 'You are not having any fun, why you don't just get up and go to your barracks.' I was obedient to that voice...

"I was running from God, but you cannot run from God. He knows where you are. While I was in the military as a soldier, I attended a club, and I heard a voice saying, 'You are not having any fun, why you don't just get up and go to your barracks.' I was obedient to that voice.

"Because I was a backslider, I knew it was the Lord. I knew the Lord was drawing me, but I was not 100% ready to give God my heart yet. During that week, a fellow soldier (she had a former reputation of cussing like a sailor but had just recently become saved) invited me to a revival service that was going on that week. I told her 'No,' but she was so persistent, and I finally said 'yes' on that Thanksgiving night. I only said, 'yes' to get her off my back and to make my boyfriend jealous."

Lady Trina turns back to the Lord and here continues to tell her story.

"During that same revival service I attended, there were lots of young people, and my future husband was among them. We were on the same Church van taking us back and forth to Church."

Lady Trina's future husband and Pastor had recently come back to God two months prior than I had.

"We were just young people having fun, loving one another, and so grateful to be saved. Eventually, we got to know each other by courtship. There was a time, we both went to the Pastor of the Church we attended, and George told our Pastor that he wanted me to be his Wife. Our Pastor made an announcement to the Church congregation that George and I were engaged! Everyone was happy for us, and it will be over 43 years married next month. Time has flashed by, and it does not seem that long," Lady Trina says as she reflects.

"In our effort to get to know this beautiful Pastor's Wife even more, the interview continues. She continues to answer from her heart."

Leading Lady Trina, did you ever envision that you would one day be a Pastor's Wife, and was the role what you thought it would be?

"No, it never entered my mind. I never thought about being a First Lady; I just wanted to be saved. I was so happy that Jesus had given me another chance for salvation. When I was in my sins, I told God, if I ever get back to Him (as saved again), I do not want to be in and out of the Church – in other words playing Church. I meant that from my heart. I wanted to be sincere and genuine about salvation."

How long have you served in the role of a Pastor's Wife, and how did it come to be?

"As of this present time, we have served as Pastor and Wife for 26 years. We left our former home Church congregation in 1995. My former Pastor was the district Superintendent (a Pastor who oversees more than one Church), and a Church was opening. Our Superintendent told my husband to go and preach at that Church on that Sunday. When my husband returned, my former Pastor gave him the privilege to become the Pastor there without me knowing. He kicked us out! I had plans to stay and let my husband go to the new Church, but my Pastor's Wife said, 'No, you cannot do that. You must go be a help to your husband.'"

Would you mind sharing some of the challenges you have encountered during your time as a first Lady?

So many things, she starts out by answering, "I am somewhat shy and do not like to be upfront. I prefer to be in the background, but God has a way to put you in situations to bring you out. God has a sense of humor!" Another thing, she suddenly notes, "Comparing yourself with other first ladies. That is a big mistake! God made only one of me, and there are no xerox copies. (Yes, I love me!)

"I can also relate to Moses' testimony when he told God that he was not eloquent in speech. God has helped me when I get up before the congregation, and he will put His words in your mouth. See Exodus 4:14-16 (KJV). Lady Trina continues, "It is human nature to want to please people, and YOU CANNOT, SO STOP IT! Just please God! I have learned to give my weakness to God and have learned to be authentic and be myself."

148

And Lady Trina, we speculate that in your role, all is not a challenge. Please, share with us your more joyful side of being the **Pastor's Wife.**

> *I have learned to give my weakness to God and have learned to be*

"Some of the joys I have experienced since becoming a First Lady are backsliders coming to Jesus and being born again, becoming God's sheep. Also, seeing our Church babies grow up

> *Some of the joys I have experienced since becoming a First Lady are backsliders coming to Jesus and being born again, becoming God's sheep...*

and become young adults, starting their career by going to college or the military, getting married, working a good job legally, and just being an overall good citizen." Lady Trina continues in this vein, "Also, it brings joy when the Church shows love to us on "**SPECIAL DAYS,**" such as: "**Sweetheart Day**" – (when the Church congregation makes an effort to organize a special day to honor the Pastor's Wife with their kind tributes, gifts, and offering), and the "**Pastor and Wife's Anniversary**" (a Special Day set aside to honor both the Pastor and his Wife for their love and dedication to the ministry – a thank you day), to show their appreciation to us as their leaders."

As we are introduced to the woman of God that stands lovingly beside her husband, the Pastor, we would like to know a little about all the places she has served before, during, or after she stepped into her role as the first Lady. Her position involves so much more than just sitting there looking pretty!

"Since I accepted Jesus Christ as my Lord and Savior, I have served as Usher President, Kindergarten, Primary, and the Adult Women's Sunday School Teacher, Sunday School secretary, Drama, Skit, and Play Director, Auxiliary Fundraiser Organizer, Teacher of the Bible Band (Bible Study Class), and The Young Women Christian Council teacher. I have been the president of the District Deacon and Minister Wives President." Lady Trina has been the cook, janitor, greeter, on the

149

witness team, the program typist, a part of the local and district-wide choir, the youth choir director, and respectfully the list goes on.

"Organizer of the Annual Rainbow Tea and mistress of ceremony. I have learned to do whatever my hands find to do. I try to do it with all of my heart." "And whatever you do, do it heartily, as to the Lord and not to men, knowing that from the Lord you will receive the reward of the inheritance; for[a] you serve the Lord Christ" Colossians 3:23-24 (NKJV)."

> I have learned to do whatever my hands find to do…I try to do it with all of my heart. "And whatever you do, do it heartily, as to the Lord and not to men, knowing that from the Lord you will receive the reward of the inheritance; for[a] you serve the Lord Christ" Colossians 3:23-24 (NKJV).

Lady Trina adds, "It does not matter if you are a First Lady, be a servant of the Lord and do ministry!"

[NICHELLE'S NOTE – 9] *Sharing the continual list of responsibilities a Pastor's Wife has is not to glorify her or to place an improper emphasis on a soul's works. We, who read our Bible, should understand that everything we have needed for salvation was finished by Christ!*

I felt it important to tear down the in-Church stereotype that the First Lady's role is so much less than it is. I hope as the backstories of these beautiful women of God are read that many will see that her role is so much more than many realize and recognize! Most Leading Ladies serve as unto the Lord, and they are involved in the ministry (beside their husband, the Pastor) in more ways than you know. God will get the glory as they do it for God, but it does not hurt when a congregation keeps her in their daily prayers and look to see where they can support her and from a pure heart be willing to help lighten the load and list of things she or her husband is expected to do.

150

We do hope that every first Lady has a balance in her life. We sincerely hope that the Wife of the Pastor has and takes the time to have hobbies and extracurricular activities that she enjoys from time to time.

> *During this COVID-19 or pandemic tribulation time, I believe God is giving everyone time to get their heart's right so we can be rapture ready when he returns, just like He did for the "Five Wise Virgins who had oil in their lamps." (See Matthew Chapter 25). Jesus is on His way back for those who are ready for His return. Get right, people, and let's go home!*

To this, Lady Trina says she walks at least three times a week minimum but aims for five days a week. She does this with other great friends of hers; one of these is also a Pastor's Wife. First Lady Curry also says, "I make candy or money leis for special occasions such as graduations, baby diaper cakes (baby showers), crafts for Christmas, baked goods, etc."

What have you learned as the first Lady that you wish you had known before you stepped into the role?

"You cannot do everything. You must delegate! One of my leaders told me to, 'Know the difference between Church work and ministry.' That leader continued, 'It's not your fault if members decide to leave the Church for whatever reason. Don't feel guilty or bad because Church people are going to do what they want to do.'

> *You cannot do everything you must delegate! One of my leaders told me to 'Know the difference between Church Work and Ministry...*

As we come to the end of the chapter in this book alone, we know that God will fulfill his promises in and through Lady Trina's life. She wanted to say this to us.

"During this COVID-19 or pandemic tribulation time, I believe God is giving everyone time to get their heart's right so we can be rapture ready when he returns, just like He did for the "Five Wise

Virgins who had oil in their lamps." (See Matthew Chapter 25). Jesus is on His way back for those who are ready for His return. Get right, people, and let's go home!

FAVORITE SCRIPTURE:

"I will bless the Lord at all times: his praise shall continually be in my mouth" Psalm 34:1 (KJV). And (Psalm 91) God has brought me from a mighty long way, and I won't forget from where I came from, and Psalm 91 has taken me through this pandemic. I am learning to dwell in my secret place in the Lord, having my own personal revival all by myself.

FAVORITE SONG(S):

I'm So Glad That The Lord Saved Me (Traditional) and *Jesus Saves* by Tasha Cobb

DREAM VACATION(S):

Hawaii and I would love to re-visit Frankfurt, Germany

Thank you, Lady Trina, for allowing us to get to know you better. We have, for you, just one more question. At the end of your life, on earth, how would you want people to remember you?

"That I was a faithful servant of God and to my leadership."

CHAPTER SIXTEEN

Lady Monique Townsend/Connecticut

*M*ay I introduce to you **Lady Monique Townsend**. When you first meet Lady Monique, you first notice her warm and welcoming smile; and with her perceptive eyes, she seems to look past your presented persona and right into your soul - discerning all that is in your heart.

I asked her to say something to all of those who would read this book. Lady Monique, what would you want other Pastors' wives and others to hear from you? What message would you want to leave for them, right here, from you? Lady Monique is a woman with an expertise with words, and this is one of the sentiments she wanted to leave with the readers.

The admonishment above comes from a Woman of God who says she had no idea or interest in being a First Lady. She goes on to say, "I was only interested in pursuing my college career and obtaining a government job." God had a different plan for Lady "M" because, at the point of this writing, she has now served over 30 years, beside her husband as a Pastor's Wife.

REAL

REALIZE that you are representing Christ.

EVOLVE, change as the Holy Spirit and Holy Word directs and instructs.

ACCENTUATE the good works that God has done in mankind and for mankind.

LOVE all, liberate bonds and live for CHRIST.

Wanting to know more of her story, I began by asking how she came to have a relationship with Jesus Christ. First Lady "M" responds.

"My family introduced Jesus to me as a teenager, and I prayed that I would accept Him as Lord. I was in my twenties when I received the manifestation of Holy Spirit with the evidence of speaking in tongues; during a revival."

154

The interview continues: How did you meet your husband, the Pastor?

"I met my husband at a sporting event I was attending with my brother."

Was he Pastoring or ministering before you met him? (Please explain)

"No, my husband was not a Pastor or minister. He was an athlete with a thriving future. We later stepped into a ministry that had previously been established to become that congregation's leading couple."

Lady Monique continues, "The role of First Lady was worse than I thought because the membership (we Pastored) was divided. Some thought my husband and I were too young, and then some did accept us as leaders. However, over the years, the attitude changed as the Bible was taught and more of them became sincere partakers of the Word of God."

> *The role of First Lady was worse than I thought because the membership (we Pastored) was divided. Some thought my husband and I were too young, and then some did accept us as leaders. However, over the years, the attitude changed as the Bible was taught and more of them became sincere partakers of the Word of God.*

In what capacity (roles, auxiliaries, jobs) have you served in and around your Church congregation?

"As a First Lady, usually you step up when there is a void. My main role is a position of prayer. I have served in many areas: Choir director, Bible Study Teacher, Soloist, Cook, Janitor, Greeter, and Church Bus Driver. I have also served as a representative to state and national conventions within my Church denomination."

She continues to speak on her service outside of the four walls of the edifice, "Senior Care Home visits for prayer or song services, also home visits to the sick and homebound." Lady Monique has also done community work for pregnancy, foster care, and adoption agencies.

155

Lady Monique, what are some of the challenges you have encountered during your time as the Pastor's Wife?

"I have had the challenge of staying subject to the Holy

> *I have had the challenge of staying subject to the Holy Spirit when I see or know the enemy is targeting and causing schism (division) in the Church.*

Spirit when I see or know the enemy is targeting and causing

> *I wish that I had known before, that all who are or who were in the Church were not in Christ. I wish I had known that some suffering just goes along with ministry.*

schism (division) in the Church.

"Keeping my eyes on Christ and not the circumstances; being

prayerful when the funds are low, when sickness comes, and

even when haters are just hating. Most important is **knowing** that it is an act of the enemy!

I wish that I had known before, that all who are or who were in the Church were not in Christ. I wish I had known that some suffering just goes along with ministry."

Lady "M" in your 50 years beside your husband, in Christ's service, please tell us some of the joys you have experienced in the role of the Pastor's Wife?

"Some of the joys I have experienced are:

1. Seeing a young convert develop in the Word of God and become a true witness for the kingdom and a voice of righteousness.
2. Being appreciated for who "I AM" in Christ. Being encouraged and prayed for by the Church Family.

Lady Monique is represented in her chapter with the "White Magnolia" flower. In her spare time, she enjoys such extracurricular activities as calligraphy, journaling, making flower pens, cookbooks, corsages, scrapbooking, and engaging in fit calisthenics.

156

FAVORITE SCRIPTURE:

Proverbs 3:5-6, "This scripture reminds me that God is in charge of all, and I must acknowledge Him in everything, and He will keep me in anything," Lady Monique says.

FAVORITE COLOR:

Purple

FAVORITE SONG(S):

I Sing Because I'm Happy by Kirk Franklin and *Because of Who you Are* by Martha Munizzi

If your Church congregation were to send your husband and yourself on an all-expense-paid vacation to anywhere, where would you want to go?

I would like to go to Africa to see all the sights and wonders of the Mother Land. I would like to view the highest mountain, safari lands, pyramids, and exotic animals – gnu, civet, crane, kudu, and other interesting facts found only there.

First Lady Monique, at the end of your life on earth, how would you want people to remember you?

I would like to be remembered as a Godly woman who loved "to love," A person with a Spirit of generosity, integrity and total commitment to Christ. Remembered as "One never without a smile.

"I would like to be remembered as a Godly woman who loved "to love," a person with a Spirit of generosity, integrity, and total commitment to Christ. I would like to be remembered as, "One never without a smile."

What an honor it was to have met this Pastor's Wife! Indeed, she is one of God's jewels, and like jewelry under a bright spotlight, her smile certainly gleams! I love you, Lady Monique!

'CHOSEN'

*O*nce upon a time, as most storybook romances go, you met your husband, and he was thrilled to meet you. The variables in each of these chapters are not all the same, but the Truth anyhow is that **HE WANTED YOU!**

You both had some interest in each other, and then there was further interaction. And then, eventually, *a choice was made.* There had to be some sort of attraction. You two are now married. Y'all said, "I DO" at some point, the ring on your finger says to all that **HE CHOSE YOU!**

I realize you had to choose him back for a wedding and marriage to ensue, but let us just go back and focus on the fact that **HE CHOSE YOU!**

He could have chosen Sally; Margot was consistently in his face; Dolores was fasting and praying. Look here now, I'm just saying… So many others yearned for that man's embrace, but it was you that he pursued and chased!

Don't forget it! Others looking at you all comprehend it. YOU were the one that he chose! No, every day is not happy, and sometimes you force a smile on Sunday, but your marriage is honorable, and there are so many who are enviable.

When you feel insecure, remember: He does not want them. **HE CHOSE YOU!**

Work it out on your knees, worship your way into God's presence, get counsel if you must, and always in God, put your full trust!

Don't give up so easily. IT IS a Spiritual battle. In Jesus' name, go ahead, and bind up that devil! Stay in God's peace and get wise counsel if you please,

You are the best one for him, and you are still the best choice! He could have chosen one of them, but instead, he made you his gem!

Others may vie for his attention, others may desire to be at his side, but that place, that entire space, is already taken BECAUSE HE CHOSE YOU!

CHAPTER SEVENTEEN

Lady Mavis Turner/Washington State

met **Lady Mavis** in Tacoma, Washington, when we were very young, and as a matter of fact, we were yet, giving birth to children here 'n there, lol. One significant memory was being invited over to the Turner's house for their toddler son's birthday party. Always so kind, hospitable, and just plain ole down to Earth. I remember lots of laughter and fun! The children, of course, were having such a great time running around and playing.

If I had ever met God's people these, were them. I remember meeting her mother as she visited Washington from Memphis. This woman was an anointed musician and played beautifully on the piano. This was and yet is a singing family! I have not heard them sing in years as I moved away, but they are gifted with beautiful voices that harmonize to the glory and honor of our "Great God!"

Lady Mavis and I have not seen each other personally in years, but when we talked over the phone, and she allowed me to interview her for this purpose, it was very easy to pick up where we had left off. We are now the mothers of adult children and even grandmas, but I am glad to say that we are yet friends!

So, come along with me. Use your 'Sanctified Imagination' as we travel to the beautiful Pacific Northwest and Meet Lady Mavis. *'I introduce to some and present to others.'*

"Well, you know Mom was a pianist in Memphis, and back then, children stayed with their moms. I went everywhere she went. She was playing for a Baptist Church primarily, and that is where we attended, but there was a time, we went to Eastside Church of God in Christ, and Mom was playing for the choir. I was only twelve years old, but I had heard stuff about the Church of God in Christ, namely that they acted unseemly! So, even when Mom and I had gone there, I would never go into the building, believing what I had previously heard.

163

"This specific occasion was a Gospel Concert. I happened to see some of my friends from school who were coming to this event and COGIC, as well. They were calling me a "chicken" because I wouldn't go in. So, I went in, and it changed my whole life!

> *I found myself on my knees, saying Lord, please help me, save me, I wanna be saved, I want to be new! I was willing and ready to give up to the Lord!*

"Whatever these people had, I wanted too! The Spirit of Praise 'n Worship was in this place. The joy, the dancing before the Lord! The 'Shouting unto God with voices of Triumph,' this was 'Joy,' and I wanted that joy too! *What exactly is going on here?* I thought.

"They prayed for me, had the young people there to come around, and the Holy Spirit came upon me in such a blessed way. I began to rejoice as well. I found myself on my knees, saying Lord, please help me, save me, I wanna be saved, I want to be new! I was willing and ready to give up to the Lord!

"I began to speak in other tongues as the Spirit gave utterance. See Acts 2. This was a different type of experience I had not ever had before!

WOW! I love it! That Holy Ghost fire revival experience! It certainly is a different type of experience; I can attest to that!

Now, I remember when your family and my family were a part of the Eastside Church of God in Christ Church family of Tacoma, Washington. I remember your husband was a young minister and you the young minister's Wife.

[NICHELLE'S NOTE – 10] *The Pastor's Wife of Eastside COGIC - Lady Mary Davis, was our Pastor's Wife at that time. She is also one of the 'Women of God' (specifically) that this book,*

MEET THE PASTOR'S WIFE, is dedicated to. Follow the Table Of Contents to the formal dedication page and read briefly about her.

Please share with us how you met your husband? I understand you two have now been married for twenty-nine years. That is a Blessing!

"We both went to WSU (Washington State University). I lived in the dorm there, and my roommates were Christians. It was also a co-ed dormitory. I hung around like-minded people; we were young people that were living for the Lord. There was a couple of times my husband and I were around each other, but it was just in passing. We really did not have our minds on each other at the time. Yes, we were both seriously "Saved," but we had other love interests at the time.

"We had mutual friends in Church that agreed that he and I would make a great couple because of our heart for God, and after a long string of events, we did become the best of

> *We had mutual friends in Church that agreed that he and I would make a great couple because of our heart for God, and after a long string of events, we did become the best of friends.*

friends. I still wasn't looking at him in any other way as a friend, and I was trying to help him make a love connection with this young Lady he had a crush on.

"It was later that he told me that he liked me because I was fun, lol. Fast forward, some time elapsed, and one day EARLY, he comes to the door of my apartment and says that the Lord has spoken to him and that I was the one he was to marry. There is more to the story, and the rest is history!

"I had taken other gentlemen to my Pastor (Davis) to meet to give his blessing, and Howard was the only somebody Pastor had approved of for me. He is like my father. He looked out for other young ladies and me. He had met Howard before and liked him for me immediately. He was right. It's already been 29 years. Thank you, Jesus!

"I was not surprised that my husband would be a Pastor; it was in him the calling, and he loves the people of God so much. My husband is an intercessor. We are not re-located back in the Washington area, but he Pastored in Memphis, TN.

Lady Mavis, what have been some of the challenges you have encountered in this specific role?

"Getting the people to come in was a challenge. Sometimes it was just the family that was present. I remember there were times the offering was only what we put in. It was a challenge when you wanted you to pray for them, but they would not come on in. We wanted them to be plugged in. You're in the position, wanting to get them to come in and make that total commitment to the Lord. So many of them would seem to want to commit about the time it looked like they might be going to jail or so sick, but otherwise, some would not avail themselves to the Lord. My husband and I had a heart for the people.

"We wanted them to know that they could have joy, patience, and peace of mind with Jesus. There were those that expressed that they were coming, that they would be to the house of the Lord and come to Jesus, but so many were fake or phony, still wanting to go to the club or smoked, not willing to commit themselves to the Lord."

Lady Mavis then referred to the scripture: "But seek ye first the kingdom of God, and his righteousness; and all these things shall be added unto you" Matthew 6:33 (KJV).

166

Yes, Ma'am, that's God's Word, we have all got to seek God first, and He certainly will add to us.

In and around the Church, what roles have you served in, Lady Mavis?

"Singing, the choir director, hearing the word of God, ushering, I have enjoyed being in the children's Church (my favorite) children's choir director."

Is there anything you like to do outside of the four walls of the Church, activity-wise?

"I enjoy watching those old "classic" 1940 – 1965 black 'n white movies — those old movies with no cursing. I love the movies that make you laugh, clean comedies."

What would you want people to remember about you when this life here on earth is over?

"I would want people to remember that I was a God-fearing woman that loved people from her heart; and that I did so unconditionally no matter what they came from or what they had done in life. I want people to see that I saw something good in every person and that with loving-kindness, better was seen than the bad.

Lady Mavis, please leave some wise advice for other First Ladies.

> *I would say to Pastors' wives to be encouraged, never let the enemy get your mind to wandering. Because when the enemy gets your mind, he is a deceiver, and he enhances insecurity.*

"Know your husband! God put you together, and you are to pray for your husband that the enemy will keep his hands off him and that any stronghold will be broken. I have never had to worry about certain things. My husband loves the Lord. I would

167

say to Pastors' wives to be encouraged, never let the enemy get your mind to wandering. Because when the enemy gets your mind, he is a deceiver, and he enhances insecurity.

"I would encourage women to stay prayerful for your husband and the ministry. God won't put more on you than what He has enabled you to bear if he has been faithful all these years. Don't allow stuff that's not there to invade in your mind about your husband. Be that person that stands by your husband. God will show you, listen, and then have God direct you toward things you must move on. Don't get emotional and upset over things.

"What's done in the dark will come to the light! Pastor's wives, you must be wise. Don't bring women around your men. Meet up at the Church, at the Church dinner.

"Have the blood of Jesus cover his walk, mind, and heart. Be diligent daily to pray without ceasing. Stop gossiping. Start praying. What can we do together to make this better? This is a good question to ask yourself within your marital relationship.

"My husband and I live a simple and humble life. We don't go above our means. We have learned to agree to disagree about some things. We don't always agree. We don't have arguments; we have heated discussions.

> *I went through a dark place after the loss of a child, years ago. I went through an anxiety place. My husband never said, 'I'm done with you.' He never said one thing about breaking the deal.*

"Concerning "Us," There's no deal-breaker for us! We are one. If I am going through something, he is going through something too because we are one. It's a "We" thing.

"I went through a dark place after the loss of a child, years ago. I went through an anxiety place. My husband never said, 'I'm done with you.' He never said one thing about breaking the deal.

[NICHELLE'S NOTE – 11] *Unfortunately, the Turners went through a tragedy, and their eldest child is now with the Lord, but through it all, God has kept them.*

"I didn't go to Church for a long time. I was accused of certain things by the saints concerning the death of my son. I had to come to myself and apologize to my husband. In my anguish, I acted angrily toward him.   He yet stood by me, even with my anger issues, and I stood by him during his low period. 'For better, for worse' were the vows we once made to each other. Through it all, "We are one."

Lady Mavis, I do thank you for sharing with us even some of your most hurtful moments. The passing of a child is not an easy situation to go through. My family has had to bury a child, too, and yes, it is one of the hardest things to do. We aren't all in the same shoes, and all of us have handled grief differently, but the Blessing on each of our journeys is the joy of knowing "JESUS!"

May I say for me that "If it had not been for the Lord on my side, where would I be?" Surely, so many of us could've lost our minds, but God! He kept us! Glory to God, and as a matter of fact, grief is such a funny animal – so to speak, and the Truth is that God continues to keep us! Hallelujah!

Lady Mavis' FAVORITE THINGS:

FAVORITE COLOR:

Blue

FAVORITE SONG:

More Than Anything **by Anita Wilson**

FAVORITE SCRIPTURE:

"Now unto Him who is able to do exceedingly abundantly above all that we ask or think, according to the power that works in us" Ephesians 3:20 (NKJV).

CHAPTER EIGHTEEN

Lady Christine Daniels/Texas

am a member too. A member like everybody else is! I can just take a seat wherever; I can take a seat back. When you are the Pastor's Wife, it's work! I am a working Pastor's Wife!

These are the confident words of First Lady **Christine Daniels**, a Texas Pastor's Wife. At the point of our conversation, Lady Daniels had been through a health battle, but God had blessed her recovery, and she was excited to "Run On" with God further on life's journey!!

I introduce to some and present to others, a mother of four adult children, in a marriage that has spanned 40 ½ years and counting, a member of the great Mt. Hope Baptist Church. You will be blessed. This First Lady is a feisty one!

"I am a doer! I wear many hats, and whatever needs to be done, Christine is there!

> *I show hospitality and love. I make them comfortable where they can talk, and they can open up to me if they have a problem. I say to them, 'Hey, let's go to the Word.'*

"Because (by God's grace), I am a servant. I don't just sit! Who am I? I am an encourager, and when the ladies see what I am doing, they follow. I have so many daughters and sons in the world. It had been prophesied that I would be a mother of many.

"I show hospitality and love. I make them comfortable where they can talk, and they can open up if they have a problem. I say to them, 'Hey, let's go to the Word.'

So, bless the lord, you've been married for over 40 years! Congratulations, beautiful! Please, tell us how you met your husband?

173

"When we met, neither of us was saved. We met at the club, and as it was, I got saved before he did. It was a process for us both to really get that real relationship with the Lord. We had both been raised up going to Church; once I got saved, my husband would only go to Church to satisfy me.

"It was one Wednesday, and there was a revival in Corsicana (Texas); God touched him, and he's never been the same since!" I can hear the emotion in her voice. "I know, I know, God touched him! God touched him, and he's never been the same since! We know who holds us in his hands!

> It was one Wednesday, and there was a revival in Corsicana (Texas); God touched him, and he's never been the same since!" I can hear the emotion in her voice. "I know, I know, God touched him! God touched him, and he's never been the same since! We know who holds us in his hands!

"Within the Church, he started to teach Sunday School, and in about a year or so was called to the ministry; and six months or so later, God opened doors, and he became the Pastor. At this point, he has been Pastoring for 28 years."

Lady Daniels, you are a 'doer of God's word,' so please tell us of what your hands have found to do within the Church setting there.

"I have worked in the service of food, have taught Sunday School from ages 1 – 12 years, been over the women's department, and have organized the conferences...." She reflects, *many hats* "... served in the choir, a part of praise 'n worship, over the homecoming program, greeting card ministry where I send cards to prisoners and others, and reminding people, You might fall down, but **get back up!**

Lady Daniels continues.

"I like to encourage people to "Do it heartily as unto the Lord..." Refer to Colossians 3:23 (KJV).

"Anything we do, we must do the best we can. If one can't do their best, why do it?"

All right, now let's change the perspective from one Pastor's Wife to another; what would you say to encourage another First Lady?

"Go before God and pray, encourage your husband to pray too, asking God to direct your steps. Be humble. Ask God to direct you in what to say. *'Lord, show me what to do and how to do it, and please direct my steps.'"*

Yes, ma'am, that sounds simple enough, and leadership should never forget to continually pray and to have the attitude that follows the direction of God. In this author's own opinion, both confusion and tragedy await the congregation when the leadership strays away from praying and seeking God's will.

Lady Daniels continues to speak to other First Ladies.

"It's always good to have another person above you that you can go to. You don't want to tell everybody everything. *'Lord, put a Godly person in my life that won't tell all of my business.'"*

> *"It's always good to have another person above you that you can go to. You don't want to tell everybody everything. 'Lord, put a Godly person in my life that won't tell all of*

Thank you for sharing that wisdom with us.

Please, tell us about a challenging time, as a Pastor's Wife, in your ministry.

"Well, let me first say that I'm not bossy, but I just know what they should be doing. If I see what needs to be done, I do it. I am a worker! I had to pray for myself, 'Lord, slow me down.'

"I had been employed in food service for many years, and so I know how it all is supposed to work. I was working in our Church's kitchen when one day, my husband said he needed to talk to me later on. He said basically, 'I'm gonna have to ask you to step down from working in the kitchen.'

> *Well, let me first say that I'm not bossy, but I just know what they should be doing. If I see what needs to be done, I do it. I am a worker! I had to pray for myself, 'Lord, slow me down.'*

"Whew, that got to me! I heard God say to me, 'Christine, don't be like that, don't be mad at him!'

Lady Daniels continues to tell me about the aftermath of the conversation her husband; also her Pastor had with her; it turns out God had more in store for her if she would humble herself.

"God said to me, 'You will do good things and be paid for it. What I have for you, it's gonna be BIG! Go back and smile!'"

It turns out that Lady Daniels was so known for her expertise in food service, even on the outside of the four walls of the Church. There was an organization on the outside that began to interview her for a catering job for 500 people. This would be a 3-day job that would pay in the neighborhood of $17,000.00. Because Lady Daniels submitted herself to her husband and Pastor and made every attempt to bring her attitude in prayerfully. This particular job was not to be hers, but God revealed to her the caliber of just what he could do for her if she would submit to him. God really does have the 'exceedingly abundantly above all that we could ever ask for or think' paraphrase of Ephesians 3:20 (KJV).

Let's get to know Lady Daniels some more. Here are a few of her FAVORITE THINGS:

FAVORITE SONG:

He Knows My Name by Tasha Cobbs

FAVORITE BOOK:

Arrow in My Heart by Nichelle Williams Isiah (she literally said this, lol)

(AVAILABLE ON AMAZON)

FAVORITE COLOR:

Purple

If your Church congregation were to send you and the Pastor on an all-expense-paid vacation, where would you want to go?

England, Paris, (I am simple) Austin, Houston

HOBBY/PERSONAL PAST TIME:

Doing Bible puzzles, encouraging someone

God bless you, Lady Daniels, and thank you for sharing your story!

THEY CAN'T STAND IN YOUR HEELS

Let's just tell the truth and shame the devil; one of the most envied people in the entire Church congregation is the 'Woman of God' in the 'First Lady' role, but honestly and truthfully: They can't *stand in your heels*.

Many don't want what you go through from Sunday to Sunday, and they merely just see you as this spotlighted celebrity. Don't let it bother you.

Some just don't realize that it takes God's Anointing to *stand in your heels.* There is "God's Grace" behind your smile; and God's *"Joy" that gives you strength.* In those heels, you stand tall. Those heels, for you only, were meant. "Lady," may God keep you *standing in those heels*.

Steadfast, because you pray and *lasting* because you fast, giving God all the praises, with *hinds' feet in high places.*

Walk tall, *walk worthy of your vocation. Look to Jesus, the author, and finisher of your Salvation.* Those are your heels to stand and step in; yours alone, for Truth, be told:

THEY CAN'T STAND IN YOUR HEELS.

1 CORINTHIANS 15:58

PSALM 18:33

EPHESIANS 4:1

HEBREWS 12:2

NEHEMIAH 8:10

CHAPTER NINETEEN

Lady Darci Bennett/New Mexico

𝓛ong before **Ms. Darci Bennett** became a Pastor's Wife, she was on another pathway. In a backslidden condition, at some point, she had strayed away from God. Lady Darci continues with her story.

"Then, When I was about twenty, I was on my way to Church, and I heard this song on the radio, which was, *The Lord is Trying to Tell You Something.* During the altar call, the Pastor said somebody needed to come to the altar. At the time of him saying this, I found myself on the floor crying out to the Lord, and I have been running for the Lord ever since."

I asked Lady Bennett: Did you ever envision that you'd one day be a First Lady, and was it what you thought (the role) would be? Why or why not?

> *Then When I was about twenty, I was on my way to Church, and I heard this song on the radio which was, The Lord is Trying to Tell You Something. During the altar call the Pastor said somebody needs to come to the altar. At the time of him saying this I found myself on the floor crying out to the Lord, and I have been running for the Lord ever since.*

"No, in no way did I think that I would be in this position. In this position, there are a lot of things you have to bite your tongue about. You have to keep smiling and go on. I am still learning every day to be the woman that the Lord has called me to be, not a man. I have now been in this position for almost ten years, and I continue to learn from other women who are currently in this position."

Lady Darci, you told me you have now been married over thirty years, Praise the Lord. That is a blessing. Have you two ever been the senior leaders of a Church congregation before now?

"We have helped other Pastors, but this is the first time we have been in this position."

181

So, tell us, First Lady Bennett, other places, and roles you have served in the Body of Christ?

"I have served in the Hospitality department, been over the noonday prayer service, as well as participating in prison and the nursing home ministry. I also helped with communion, the children's ministry, and a teacher during Vacation Bible School. All of this was done for the Glory of God. I also enjoy walking and a little gardening."

So, you are married to a Pastor. Please, tell us how you two met?

"We met at the nightclub. I received salvation first, and then my husband accepted the Lord as his savior. The scripture is very true when it says, 'the unbelieving husband is sanctified through his Wife' Refer to 1 Corinthians 7:14 (KJV)."

Amen. Amen, your husband is now serving the Lord and Pastoring. Look at God!

Please, tell us of both the joys and challenges of being a Pastor's Wife, Lady Darci.

"The Joy that I have is just meeting different people and knowing you are doing the will of the Father."

"A challenge would be being able to deal with the different personalities and learning the women and men of God the Lord has put in our care."

Say something to all of those who will read this book. What would you want them to hear from you?

When things become hard, and some things may happen that you don't understand, just continue to pray. Prayer is the answer! We have our own personal situations to deal with, along with the congregation's problems. I just encourage you to pray and pray again. The Bible says to pray without ceasing." Refer to 1

182

"When things become hard, and some things may happen that you don't understand, just continue to pray. Prayer is the answer! We have our own personal situations to deal with, along with the congregation's problems. I just encourage you to pray and pray again. The Bible says to pray without ceasing." Refer to 1 Thessalonians 5:16-28 (KJV)**."**

Lady Darci, at the end of your life, how would you want to be remembered?

"I want to be remembered as a woman that trusted in God despite her circumstances."

Thank you, Lady Darci, for sharing with us! As we conclude this chapter, we will list a few of your FAVORITE THINGS.

FAVORITE FLOWERS:

Purple lilacs

If your Church congregation wanted to send you and your hubby on an all-expense-paid for vacation, where would you want to go?

Hawaii

FAVORITE SCRIPTURE AND WHY?

2 Corinthians 2:14. "Now thanks be unto God, which always causes us to triumph in Christ, and makes manifest the savour of his knowledge by us in every place.

"The word triumph stands out to me because whatever I go through in life, I already have the victory, and it doesn't even matter how things look. Because the greater one lives in me, I am always triumphant!"

> *The word triumph stands out to me because whatever I go through in life, I already have the victory, and it doesn't even matter how things look. Because the greater one lives in me, I am always triumphant!*

FAVORITE SONG:

Because He Lives and *Tis So Sweet to Trust in Jesus*

Lady Darci, yes, it is 'SWEET' to trust in Jesus, indeed! May God continue to bless and keep you and yours. May the blessings of the Lord be on your congregation and your Pastoral leadership alongside your husband there.

CHAPTER TWENTY

Lady Lois Marie Williams/California

$\mathcal{W}$ow, how can I explain what a Divine Blessing it is to have this opportunity to write a chapter in this book about my mama. Yes, my own biological mother. She is called **Mother Williams** by most who know her but, indeed, also "A Lady."

My mom was born and raised in San Antonio, Texas, and I was surprised to hear some of her

testimony as I gave her a phone interview. She had prayed long ago about wanting to be married to a preacher. See, I went into the interview with her for "Meet the Pastor's Wife," thinking I knew my mom and possibly could write a little of her story whether I talked with her or not, but I was wrong. She had things to say, and I did learn more than I had previously known.

My mother accepted the Lord in a Youth class being taught by the Late Leroy Duhart. She says he was teaching about a place called "Hell." My mother was convicted by this lesson and turned her heart over to the Lord. This was at the then Hebrew Church of God in Christ; the name was later changed to Healing Temple Church. She still remembers the address: 1908 Dakota Street in San Antonio. That address would be the location of a lot of firsts for my mother and dad as well.

My mom says that their Church had tarrying services often. For those of you who don't know what those are, they are a time of praying, waiting, earnestly crying out to the Lord; seeking the Lord for the baptism of the Holy Spirit with the following of a new prayer language (tongues as the Spirit gives utterance. Refer to Acts 2:4

(KJV) "And they were all filled with the Holy Ghost, and began to speak with other tongues, as the Spirit gave them utterance" Acts 2:4 (KJV).

It was one of those "Tarrying services" where my mother was filled with the Holy Spirit! She was a teenager, sixteen years of age.

As most of us know, San Antonio is host to military bases, such as Lackland AFB, and Randolph AFB, and Fort Sam Houston, TX, where my dad was stationed. I must sneak this in here. My  dad, a native of California and a Christian, had been praying about getting married, and he had asked God to give him a Wife. It was shortly after that when he was drafted into the Army. My dad says he thought he would just put the thought of finding a Wife (Proverbs 18:22) aside until he returned from military duty in approximately four years. My dad didn't realize at the time that God was merely answering his prayer. He was sending him to, yes, serve his country as a military medic, but he was also going to meet his Wife!

I will make this story short, for the sake of the amount of paper it would take to tell it all, but he was attending Church service (as did lots of other soldiers), that were soldiers there in that area. My father got her address, and I am told that they were pen pals for four years. Needless to say, they got married and relocated to California (went by Greyhound bus), and I am their firstborn; praise the Lord!

As time goes by, my dad is a minister fellowshipping at the Church congregation where my beloved late paternal grandpa Pastored. He gets a call from a local late elder and evangelist who has been meeting in a San Joaquin Valley town, approximately an hour from where we lived. He has been running revivals, and there was a group of attendees coming. He calls my dad and says that God has not called him to Pastor this group of people but asks my dad (Pastor James Phillip Williams) if he would pray about coming to be a Pastor to them.

My mom says that she initially did not want to move. My dad was pretty comfortable where he was as well, but God had given him the confirmation to go.

[NICHELLE'S NOTE – 12] *You know, I had to be about four years old when we moved from the town I was born to the place I was raised; yet I remember a truck being packed and another Church gentleman (Elder Turner) helping my father. I was too young then to realize that my parents were answering the call of the Lord.*

If I ever learned anything from my mom and dad, who were also my Pastor and First Lady, it was *faithfulness*! There have been many challenges over the years, and many I saw with my own eyes. It has not been often, but I have seen my mom cry over certain things. My dad is pretty quiet-natured, yet he has endured many things that God has brought them through.

I asked him several times as a child, "Daddy, have you ever thought about moving, giving up the Church?" He answered, "Yes, I have, but God has never told me to leave." *Faithful!*

My mom became a Pastor's Wife in 1972 (you do the math) as my dad obeyed God and became a Pastor. To date, and I give God the praise, my parents have been married for 55 years and counting. To God be the glory! In their ministry, there have always been just a faithful few. I, over the years, have seen many souls come in, accept Jesus, become faithful in the congregation, and then pass on. The victory is that they passed on with Christ in their heart. There had been a change.

Mama and Daddy are not *spring chickens* anymore, but God is keeping them, and God has sent some very faithful people who are there at the Los Banos Church and keep the ministry moving. I must give a **WRITTEN SHOUT OUT** to the couple who have been faithful there for years. They have been and continue to be there for their Pastor 'n Wife and the entire congregation, and I must say THANK YOU GOD for the congregation there as well. Los Banos Church of God in Christ is dear to the heart of God.

I asked Mama what she would want to say to other Pastor's wives reading this book, she said, "Be faithful, and God will bless you. Serving the Lord will pay off after a while."

Mother Williams' FAVORITE SCRIPTURES:

Hebrews 12:14. "Follow peace with all men, and holiness, without which no man shall see the Lord."

Isaiah 35:8. "And an highway shall be there, and a way, and it shall be called The way of holiness; the unclean shall not pass over it; but it shall be for those: the wayfaring men, though fools, shall not err therein."

I give a personal 'THANK YOU' to my forever Pastor and First Lady.

In your prime, you held the standard of Jesus Christ high before my sisters and me. You trained us up and did not sway. You stood firm, spanked our behind, if necessary – thank you! You had lived a Christian lifestyle before us and kept the Word of God in our face, and taught us to pray. Daddy, I still remember you coming home from work, saying hello, and then going to your bedroom. From outside

189

the door, I could hear the faint sound of your voice as you talked to God. Mama, I remember how busy you stayed, helping and doing for people, and I can't say I remember you ever opting out of Church unless you'd just had a baby. I love the fellowshipping of the Saints. I guess I got that from you!

Thank you both!

Thank you, Pastor and Lady Williams, for showing me what faithfulness looks like!

CHAPTER TWENTY – ONE

Lady Patricia Tramil/Tennessee

t was years ago while living in the State of Tennessee and living on Fort Campbell, that I had the honor of meeting **Mother Patricia Tramil**. This was the House of Praise Church. If you didn't know her, it would be hard to miss her. She greets you with this big smile, and she has a big beautiful singing voice that fills the atmosphere with praise to our God. Now, it has been years since I have personally seen Mother Tamil, but I would venture to say that she is still: "On the Battlefield for my Lord."

Mother Tramil is what we call the "District Missionary." Mother Tramil is a wise and Spiritual-seasoned woman that oversees the Women's departments over more than one Church. Trust me; this is only one of the hats that she has and is wearing now. Much has happened in her life since I last saw her, and here, we will visit her life's events as much as we can. Here goes the interview.

Mother Tramil, God bless you! First, I'd like to express my condolences regarding the passing of your husband – Superintendent Robert Tramil. I remember him as being very jovial and kind. It has been four years now, but I have not personally given you my condolences. Why don't we start there? How did you come to meet Pastor Tramil?

"Well, after I had come back to the Lord, the Church I was attending was quite away from where I was living. I decided to change Churches. I was singing with this singing group: "The Blalock Singers," and we sang that day. I had seen him earlier, he was helping to park cars, and I assumed he was one of the deacons of the Church.

"At the end of the service, one of the mothers there began to introduce him to a few single sisters there; I don't know the reason, but she never introduced him to me. That was fine with me because I really had my focus on the Lord. I found out later that he had been asking about me. He got my phone number and one day gave me a call. We had phone conversations for about a month when he asked if he could come to visit me.

"He showed up, dressed in a 3-piece suit on a Saturday, and he had a brand-new car. When I saw him, I said, 'Oh, you're that deacon.' He says, "No, I am Elder Tramil."

"Things went well between us. We enjoyed pleasant conversations and laughter. He asked if I would officially date him. I said yes. He had brought with him a bottle of Chloe perfume and a Zebra plant," she giggles, "and yes, we did eventually get married on November 17, 1984.

> *He passed away when we had been married for thirty-three years, and yes, I miss him.*

"He passed away when we had been married for thirty-three years, and yes, I miss him. I had this list before God concerning a husband, and God gave me everything I had on that list, except preacher! I didn't want a preacher. We both laugh about it."

May I ask why you didn't want to marry a Preacher?

"I thought they were too righteous. It never crossed my mind to be with a preacher. The work, the Wife on the backburner."

194

Mother Tramil speaks on.

"But God had a plan for my life! I learned that I was an asset to him, and I was to help him."

So, you and your late husband are the founders of the "House of Praise Church." I have been there many times before and had some good fired-up Church there. Can you tell me a little bit of how you all got started?

"The year was 1990, that he became a Pastor – the Lord has been dealing with him to become a Pastor. When he announced it, that's when I heard it too! When we got home, I said, 'what?' I wanted to make sure he wasn't stepping out in his flesh. We officially started the "House of Praise" in 1991.

Yes, I was forty-two years old when I became pregnant with my son. A great while earlier, I had had a miscarriage, and I had said, 'If I don't have a baby by age thirty- six then that's ok. I thought I couldn't have children.

"The first services were in my living room with the grandchildren and a brother who was coming back to the Lord. I was having a hard time breaking away from our former Church. There I was greatly involved, especially with directing the choir and the music department. It was my Bishop who said to me: 'Go, be with your husband. I know you do a lot here, but your husband is starting a Church. You need to be with him. We had grown significantly in size by 1993.

195

Please tell me about some of your challenges.

> *I had to learn that I was important to God. I used to say that God called him and not me. A mother in Zion, said 'stop saying that!' I had to learn that I had a position there and had to be his greatest supporter...*

"Number One - If I ever learned faith, it was during this process. You think you are inadequate, but God takes not knowing what to do and teaches you what to do! He doesn't call the qualified, but he qualifies the called – He will train you. You will learn how to be what He would have you to be. Like in the Bible, God saw what was in them. God looks at what is in us. God uses that for His glory! Moses was not speaking well, but he sent Aaron. God is to get the glory, and it is not to get the big head!

"Then, my husband was a wise man. He learned, and he studied. I had to learn that I was important to God. I used to say that God called him and not me. A mother in Zion said, 'stop saying that!' I had to learn that I had a position there and had to be his greatest supporter. I learned that I was the person that was a Reacher to the people. That was the role God was using me as. God gave me wisdom on how to explain and encourage the people. God taught me. I couldn't challenge everything that people were saying against my husband. My husband would listen to me when I said things the way God would tell me to say something, but then there were times, and he would shut me down when I'd start to put my flesh in it. Pastor's wives should ask God to give them women of age (Spiritually) to help when counseling is needed."

Mother Tramil, I know you have worn a lot of proverbial hats, and you have stood in many roles. Tell us about it, please.

"I started so many things in the Church. Most of the things, God would tell me what to release because my hand was in a lot. I had been trained. I worked in the finances as the treasurer. I worked as a Sunday school teacher for adults and children, women department president, choir president, over the adult choir, started youth and women's choir, started children's choir (Greater Love Choir), taught children to usher. They learned to testify. We taught them how and how to be the cook. District, state – District missionary, Clarksville, Banner March for the Women's Convention, Facilitator Pastor/wives circle, Elder's Wives Circle, to God be the Glory!"

Now, I am so excited to get to the part about your first-born son! My family had transferred from Fort Campbell, Ky (borders Tennessee and Kentucky), and I was now in another state. I had not seen nor heard from the Clarksville area in a good while. When we got the news…

"Yes, I was forty-two years old when I became pregnant with my son. A great while earlier, I had had a miscarriage, and I had said, 'If I don't have a baby by age thirty-

> There was a sister at the Church who kept kindly advising me to go take a pregnancy test, and I kept laughing at that. She said, 'First Lady, I think you should go take a pregnancy test.' I told her, 'I'm going to have a pregnancy test just to shut your mouth.' It turns out I was 3 ½ months pregnant, with cravings for watermelon and won ton soup. The Church people began to call us Abraham and Sarah, and my husband would say that he had done all that he could do.

six then that's ok. I thought I couldn't have children. I was feeling some kind of way, and I thought my sugar was dropping. There was a sister at the Church who kept kindly advising me to go take a pregnancy test, and I kept laughing at that. She said, 'First Lady, I think you should go take a pregnancy test.' I told her, 'I'm going to have a pregnancy test just to shut your mouth.' It turns out I was 3 ½ months pregnant, with cravings for watermelon and won ton soup. The Church people began to call us Abraham and Sarah, and my husband would say that he had done all that he could do." You see, my husband was sixteen years older than me. We laughed."

God brought her through. It was a normal and blessed pregnancy, and her son is now a fine young man, and I have heard he is very good on the musical keyboards and a fantastic son to her.

At the risk of sounding a little too personal, I want to say all she told me because it may encourage somebody reading this. Mother Tramil said that she gave birth by C-section and that the doctor told her afterward that he had to work through a great amount of scar tissue in her uterus. He was amazed that she had become pregnant at all. Hallelujah! God had done what He does, performed a miracle named Jared. Lady Tramil, the co-founder of House of Praise, had been married 11 years when she had her first child. God is good!

This Lady Founder then goes on to talk about Pastors and their wives making time for each other. Let's read on.

"You're so caught up into Church stuff and children. You've got to make time for each other! Priorities changed once the baby came. He and I were passing each other like two ships in the night. He was building the Church building. Sometimes you have to tell your husband when enough is enough. I didn't bother him when he was building the house of God (House of Praise). I would make him lunch, and we'd spend a little time together, but once the Church was up and built, he was now in the habit of heading out to do something regarding the Church building; but the Church was up now. I would encourage him to spend some time with me!

"Vacations were special, twice a year. We used to be calling back, worrying about the Church, but, 'You have got to trust who you leave in charge,' said my husband. 'We'll take care of it when we get back,' he would say. We loved the mountains and seeing the changing of the leaves in Gatlinburg or another state. Always keep a relationship with your husband. Children are included, but they shouldn't supersede. Find some time for each other in between. When those children are grown, they will go on with their business. Ain't no child to get between the time you have with your spouse.

"We homeschooled my son, and there was some private school as well."

"The adjustment for me is still there. They still call me Mother and Co-founder. They still show me honor. I realize that my husband is gone, and I promote our new Pastor, and I promote our new First Lady. You can't be fearful of your position. I had been there 25 years. It's a process. Everything doesn't come to my ears now, and it doesn't have to."

Mother Tramil also shared with me about an occasion that happened in the Church where she felt hurt and offended. Please, tell us a little.

"There was a time where hurtful stuff had been said about me, and I had said nothing to

anybody about it. I had made up my mind to do nothing else in the Church. We'd had a prayer meeting, and we had a guest, a relative of a family that went to our Church. After prayer, she asked if she might have a private word with me. She told me that God had given her a Word to share with me. She said, 'The Lord said, He's not gonna even receive your praise, (if she carried what was in her thoughts out), God said He has need

of you. Your husband thinks that he chose you to be his Wife, but God chose you to be his Wife and he to be your husband. You knew how to reach out, how to cover, and how to love.'"

199

So, God sent this Word to you. God indeed knows the heart.

"Before Pastor Tramil died, God let me know my place and assignment. My husband was older than me, and he stood on old-school principles and didn't agree with certain things. Sometimes, I felt he was a little harsh. I believe God used me to sort of 'pat the fire.'"

Regarding her husband's death.

"The God part of me rejoices because I know he is gone to be with the Lord, but that spouse part of me hurts daily. Yes, when a spouse passes, you will have some loneliness. We all handle things personally. I miss sharing popcorn and ice cream with him, and it's been four years, but I just can't take my wedding rings off. My husband took great care of me. The Church's building was paid off five years after moving in, as well as our house. My husband was wise and took care to be a good steward over what God had blessed us with."

FAVORITE SCRIPTURE:

"Therefore, my beloved brethren, be ye steadfast, unmovable, always abounding in the work of the Lord, forasmuch as ye know that your labor is not in vain in the Lord" 1 Cor. 15:58 (KJV).

FAVORITE COLOR:

Purple

MY CHAPTER - IN CONCLUSION

Why Did I Write a Book About The Pastor's Wife?

$\mathcal{W}$ow! Being an instrument, working to put this endeavor together has been quite an adventure of sorts! *MEET THE PASTOR'S WIFE- I Introduce To Some And Present To Others* has been both a pleasant challenge and jubilant joy! These are ALL AMAZING 'WOMEN OF GOD.' It has been such a blessing for me to have been privileged to record their testimony.

So, the question may arise, why this subject matter? What made you want to honor and explore the view of the Pastor's Wife? I will answer that question with a three-word phrase:

> *I am not a "First Lady" anymore, but I use to be. "Been there, done that." Out of respect of all my family both past and present, I won't disclose the details. This was nearly fourteen years ago now.* **BUT I REMEMBER…**

It's because I remember. Simply, **because I remember**. I am not a "First Lady" anymore, but I used to be. "Been there done that," had the stereotypical "Proverbial Heels, and the pretty laced lap scarf," if you will. Out of respect for all of my family, both past and present, I won't disclose the details of all.

It was nearly fourteen years ago now, but *I remember* being in "Another type of World," so to speak.

I remember being surrounded by people and yet feeling so lonely.

I remember "Joyously" organizing local conferences and such. I got joy out of seeking God for the theme, the speaker(s), the topics of discussion, and so on.

I was blessed in looking out across the ladies in our congregations and seeing qualities and gifting in each of them that they hadn't even yet recognized in themselves. I loved the role of encouraging and inspiring, teaching God's Word, and such. **I remember**.

A pleasant surprise to me, now all these years later, is that several of the young ladies and a few of the young men that once went to our Church remain in contact with me. They are so loving and respectful to me. I see them as my Godchildren, and I love them dearly. There are a few of them that refer to me as "Mother." One dear Lady remembers me with thoughtful gifts every birthday and many of the holidays. I have been a guest in the home of some. I am touched and blessed because of God's love being shown through them and because they didn't forget me. It is a gift to me that **I cherish**.

Here are a few more memories before I go on.

I remember the feeling of having to be flawless -- not in the way of living Holy. That is a big basic, living righteously, but being flawless in the way of -- you have no emotions (just smile). Be a flawless mom who raises flawless children and handles every situation correctly.

Watch a few "classic" episodes of *The Brady Bunch* and *Leave it to Beaver* from a few decades back. I say in jest. Those women are scripted; in real life, they have never existed. Yet, there are times when I felt like I was supposed to be flawless, and you all know that is impossible for anybody. Yes, we can live Holy (Refer 1 Peter 1:16), and we should, but I have never met anyone in ministry or not, that is not, was not, flawless.

The Joy of helping someone privately and quietly, **I remember**.

The hurtful feeling of being misunderstood is a part of a **past memory**.

The sweetness of seeing someone 'Grow in Grace' because of following God-given, Bible scripture-based instruction is **a sweet remembrance, indeed.**

204

The above is a medley of the bittersweet that I remember of my past. Notice, like in any arena of ministry, there are challenges as well, as the "So Glad About it" type circumstances. Someone might say, well, why would you even mention it if it were your past? 'You are not a Pastor's Wife anymore, and furthermore, you aren't even married at this time.'

Since this is *my chapter,* I believe I will answer that to the best of my ability and "Write the Vision…" (I have for this book) "…and make it plain…" Habakkuk 2:2-3 (KJV).

I will try to put this all in a nutshell. Though I had challenges while in the role of a Pastor's Wife, I knew that God had given me things to administrate to the Body of Christ in that local Church, where I served as a Pastor's Wife. Had my marriage have not become a part of the negative statistic, there were things I felt God had laid on my heart to do for not only Pastors' wives but women in general. Though years have gone by, as I have healed from the divorce and such, certain things have continued to come to my mind; things I should have done and could have done. Have you ever felt that you let God down?

Oh, don't get me wrong, I realize that certain things were out of my control, and I forgive myself for the places where I could have done better. For anyone reading this and you have been or are in this place that I speak of, don't allow the enemy to torment your mind! God sees and knows all, and

> As I have begun to heal from the past, there has been a great stirring concerning God's calling on my life and the gifting He has given me. Hallelujah! I thank Him for being the "Author" of MY story.

what you can't speak of publicly, he already knows. Get sound private counseling if you must, and don't you ever stop praying. God is close to the brokenhearted! Refer to Psalm 34:18.

As I have begun to heal from the past, there has been a great stirring concerning God's calling on my life and the gifting He has given me. Hallelujah! I thank Him for being the "Author" of MY story. I thank Him for the "Mind of Christ." See 1 Corinthians 2:16. I am lately feeling this great urgency to get about the things God has placed in me. I hear in my mind, now as I type, a part of an ole gospel

congregational song: "While the Blood is running warm in my veins…" As I was saying, I feel a Holy Ghost urgency to get up and do what God gave me to do. What God gave me to do may be done by other means, by another method, from the place of another position (apparently not as a Pastor's Wife), but yet God has a way. At this point, my life is not over! Going through a divorce as a Pastor's Wife is not a good thing, nothing ever to glory about, and I do not, but it is not the end-all of all things for me.

I find that God is having me do a written testimonial of my life…Hallelujah! These books are documenting the places I have been over the course of my lifetime. Now I hear the song: "How I Got Over… My Soul Looks Back and Wonders, How I Got Over…" My testimony, your testimony, these personal eyewitness accounts are going to help somebody. Somebody, (namely another 'Woman of God') …somebody who feels they are the only one, going through what they are going through…

What I have learned, I cherish. **I REMEMBER**. It helps me to pray for a First Lady when I have been there before. No, all circumstances are not the same, as you can see in each of these "Chapters." However, all have some challenges and a need to be remembered in prayer.

The scripture comes to mind, "Occupy 'til He comes…" Luke 19:30 (KJV). I have enjoyed writing for most of my life, and to now be a published author has been on my dream job list for years! It was not until the Spring of 2021 that this came to pass. thank you, Jesus! I am in my fifties at this point, but the joy is just as pleasant to me! I give God thanks for the Prophetic Ministry of Dr. Paul R. Dade of Richmond, Virginia. He continued to prophesy and say: "Now is the time forthrightly. **Now** is the time to write that book and start that business and so on." This is a paraphrase of God's words through him, for me. There was this day that I received that Word, no longer just feeling it was for somebody else, no, that Word was for me! I received it for me, in Jesus' name!

The Holy Spirit in me rose up and got me up, so to speak. God dropped into my thoughts the subject matter and Bible scripture basis for my first book, *Arrow in My Heart*, sharing a part of my motherhood journey, and soon after that, *Route Eight – Radio Check*, ministry from the driver's seat of the school bus I currently drive. By God's grace, I got my CDL (Commercial Driver's License) driving a school bus for the purpose of income when I became a single parent, and I wrote some about it.

The mini-book series that God has allowed me to start (Book #1 is now published) on simple things people can do to help be prepared BEFORE stormy times, in the natural hit. God gave me to write that in just a few hours, and more is coming on that. And now, I am writing the last chapter of **MEET THE PASTOR'S WIFE.** Thank You, Jesus!

I find that God is having me do a written testimonial of my life. Hallelujah! These books document the places I have been over the course of my lifetime. Now I hear the song, "How I Got Over... My Soul Looks Back and Wonders, How I Got Over..." My testimony, your testimony, these personal eyewitness accounts are going to help somebody. Somebody (namely another 'Woman of God') feels they are the only one going through what they are going through. It may not be everybody, but I believe and declare, in Jesus' name, that the Words of these Leading Ladies will bless MANY.

DISCLAIMER: I am not a licensed counselor (That is another of my dream jobs. I need to finish that degree.) But Bible-based counseling is out there in our communities if you need it.

While I was a Pastor's Wife, I did not host a conference for First Ladies as I yearned to do. Wow, God had given me some great ideas for the 'Women of God.' I am now in a different role. I am no longer a woman married to a Pastor; my marriage ended in divorce. That is not something I am proud of. Who marries thinking you will divorce. May God keep your marriages in a Spirit of His love! Whatever happened to my past marriage does not have to happen to yours.   For those of you who are now serving as a

Pastor's Wife, may you be strong in the Lord and the power of His might. See Ephesians. 6: 10-13.

[NICHELLE'S NOTE – 13] *If you are a woman who, like me, went through a divorce and once was married to a Pastor, my prayers are for you and your family. May God make you every whit whole, in Jesus' name. Ask God for healing from any past wounds and to help you to forgive if need be – letting go of all bitterness. Go get Christian Counseling if you need it, and **go forward**!*

God has seen my heart for these graced 'Women of God' and has given me a way to honor them. I thank Him. This book is a tribute – a spotlight, on the beautiful wives of these Pastors. God has not forgotten any of you. He sees, knows, and cares for you! Thank you all for taking the time to contribute your story. I realize your moments are valuable!

> "Finally, my brethren, be strong in the Lord, and in the power of his might. Put on the whole armor of God, that ye may be able to stand against the wiles of the devil. For we wrestle not against flesh and blood, but against principalities, against powers, against the rulers of the darkness of this world, against Spiritual

wickedness in high places. Wherefore take unto you the whole armor of God, that ye may be able to withstand in the evil day, and having done all, to stand" Ephesians 6:10-13 (KJV).

"Strength and dignity are her clothing, and she laughs at the time to come. She opens her mouth with wisdom, and the teaching of kindness is on her tongue. She looks well to the ways of her household and does not eat the bread of idleness. Her children rise up and call her blessed. Her husband also, and he praises her: "Many women have done excellently, but you surpass them all." Charm is deceitful, and beauty is vain, but a woman who fears the Lord is to be praised. Give her of the fruit of her hands, and let her works praise her in the gates" Proverbs 31: 28-31 (ESV).

May the Lord watch over you and me while we are absent one from another. In Jesus' name, AMEN.